✳ At a Glance

Sentences

✳ At a Glance

Sentences

THIRD EDITION

Lee Brandon
Mt. San Antonio College

Houghton Mifflin Company *Boston* *New York*

To Sharon

Publisher: Patricia A. Coryell
Senior Sponsoring Editor: Lisa Kimball
Senior Development Editor: Judith Fifer
Editorial Associate: Peter Mooney
Project Editor: Shelley Dickerson
Manufacturing Coordinator: Chuck Dutton
Senior Marketing Manager: Annamarie Rice
Marketing Assistant: Andrew Whitacre

Cover image: © Ablestock

Printed in the U.S.A.

Library of Congress Control Number: 2004114375

ISBN: 0-618-54226-4

456789 – MP – 09 08 07 06 05

Contents

12   The Writing Process: Paragraphs and Essays   193

✳ Preface

At a Glance: Sentences is the first-level book in the *At a Glance* series. Along with *At a Glance: Paragraphs*, *At a Glance: Essays*, and *At a Glance: Reader*, it meets the current need for succinct, comprehensive, and up-to-date textbooks that students can afford. All four books provide basic instruction, exercises, and writing assignments at the designated level, as well as support material for instructors. *At a Glance: Sentences* and *At a Glance: Paragraphs* include a transition to the next level of writing while *At a Glance: Paragraphs* and *At a Glance: Essays* end with a handbook, to which students can refer for help with sentence-level issues or for problems with mechanics. *At a Glance: Reader* presents brief writing instruction and thirty sources for reading-related writing. Each book in the *At a Glance* series can be used alone, with one of the other *At a Glance* books, or with another textbook. Two or more *At a Glance* books can be shrink-wrapped and delivered at a discount.

✳ Comprehensive Coverage

Focusing on sentence writing, *At a Glance: Sentences* covers parts of speech, subjects and predicates, phrases and clauses, sentence types, sentence combining, sentence problems (including fragments, comma splices, and run-ons), and parallel structure. It also treats specific verb, pronoun, and modifier problems, punctuation and capitalization, and spelling. The final chapter provides a bridge to the process of writing paragraphs and essays and includes student examples as well as suggestions of topics for writing.

✳ Instructional Approach

Principles, rules, and guidelines in *At a Glance: Sentences* are presented concisely and are followed immediately by appropriate examples. Exercises that offer hands-on practice and review of the material end each major section. Throughout, examples and exercises present humorous, contemporary, or culturally diverse topics that engage students' interest. When appropriate, chapters end with an exercise that asks students to write original sentences.

Changes for this edition include the following:

- new content in twenty-six exercises in sentence writing
- a new section on omissions
- a new section on sentence variety
- a new section on wordiness
- additional suggested writing topics
- the Writing Process Worksheet

✳ Support Material for Instructors

- *At a Glance* instructor website at http://college.hmco.com/devenglish/instructors: Answers to exercises; reproducible diagnostic tests and sentence-writing quizzes; sample syllabus to adopt or adapt for different course designs; PowerPoint slides.
- *At a Glance* student website at http://college.hmco.com/devenglish/students: Additional exercises; readings; instructions for writing resumes and letters of application.
- Software resources include updated Expressways 5.0 CD-ROM; interactive software that guides students as they write and revise paragraphs and essays; Houghton Mifflin Grammar CD-ROM, and the American Heritage Dictionary CD-ROM.
- Online options include Dolphinville, an online writing center, and SMARTHINKING, live online tutoring and academic support by trained e-instructors.

✳ Acknowledgments

I am profoundly indebted to the following instructors who have reviewed this textbook: Marilyn Black, Middlesex Community College; Deborah Burson-Smith, Southern University at New Orleans; Karen A. Cahill, Southeastern Community College; Iris Gribble-Neal, Eastern Washington University; Ardyce Ketterling, Bismarck State College; Tamara Kuzmankov, Tacoma Community College; David Lang, Golden Gate University; Lynette Lochausen, Colorado Mountain College; Phyllis MacCameron, Erie Community College North; Kathy Masters, Arkansas State University; Sharon Owen,

University of Texas at El Paso; Dianne Perkins, Community College of Philadelphia; John Richardson, Augusta Technical College; Judith Sinclair, Catholic University; Alice Steilder, Santa Barbara City College; Marilyn Strauss, Pace University; Steve Stremmel, American River College; Pamela A. Tackaburg, Fullerton College; and David White, Walters State Community College. Thanks also to members of the English department at Mt. San Antonio College.

I deeply appreciate the work of Nancy Benjamin of Books By Design, Mary Dalton Hoffman, and my colleagues at Houghton Mifflin Company: Lisa Kimball, Judith Fifer, Peter Mooney, Annamarie Rice, Andrew Whitacre, and Shelley Dickerson.

I am especially grateful to my family of wife, children and their spouses, and grandchildren for their cheerful, inspiring support: Sharon, Kelly, Erin, Kathy, Michael, Shane, Lauren, Jarrett, and Matthew.

Lee Brandon

✳ Student Overview

This book is designed to help you write better sentences both separately and in context.

- In Chapters 1 through 6, you'll work with understanding sentence parts, identifying kinds of sentences, putting short sentences together to show relationships, fixing groups of words that look like sentences but really are not, and balancing the parts of a sentence.
- In Chapters 7 through 11, you'll study how to make the most effective use of verbs, pronouns, adjectives and adverbs, punctuation and capitalization, and spelling.
- In Chapter 12, you'll look at the writing process as a series of steps that can carry you from stage to stage until you have produced a polished paragraph or essay.

Following are some strategies to help you make the best use of this book and to jump-start the improvement in your writing skills.

1. **Be active and systematic in learning.** Take advantage of your instructor's expertise by being an active participant in class—one who takes notes, asks questions, and contributes to discussion. Become dedicated to systematic learning: determine your needs, decide what to do, and do it. Make learning a part of your everyday thinking and behavior.

2. **Read widely.** Samuel Johnson, a great English scholar, once said he didn't want to read anything by people who had written more than they had read. William Faulkner, a Nobel Prize winner in literature, said, "Read, read, read. Read everything—trash, classics, good and bad, and see how writers do it." Read to learn technique, to acquire ideas, to be stimulated to write. Especially read to satisfy your curiosity and receive pleasure. If reading is a main component of your course, approach it as systematically as you do writing.

3. **Keep a journal.** Keeping a journal may not be required in your particular class, but whether required or not, jotting down your

observations in a notebook is a good idea. Here are some ideas for daily, or almost daily, journal writing:

- Summarize, evaluate, or react to reading assignments.
- Summarize, evaluate, or react to what you see on television and in movies, and to what you read in newspapers and magazines.
- Describe and narrate situations or events you experience.
- Write about career-related matters you encounter in other courses or on the job.

Your journal entries may read like an intellectual diary, a record of what you are thinking about at certain times. Keeping a journal will help you to understand reading material better, to develop more language skills, and to think more clearly—as well as to become more confident and write more easily so that writing becomes a comfortable everyday activity. The important thing is to get into the habit of writing something each day.

4. **Evaluate your writing skills.** Use the Self-Evaluation Chart inside the front cover of this book to list areas you need to work on. You can add to your lists throughout the entire term. Drawing on your instructor's comments, make notes on matters such as spelling, word choice, paragraph development, grammar, sentences, punctuation, and capitalization. As you master each problem area, you can check it off or cross it out.

Here is a partially filled out Self-Evaluation Chart, followed by some guidelines for filling out your own.

Self-Evaluation Chart

Spelling/ Word Choice	Paragraph Development	Grammar/ Sentences	Punctuation/ Capitalization

receive 179
a lot 181
its, it's 186
studying 184
	topic
	    sentence 185
	support 203
		fragment 56
		variety of
		    patterns 29
		comma
		    splice 64
		run-on 64
			apostrophe 170
			comma 152
			semicolon 159
			question mark
			    with
			    quotation
			    marks 152

- *Spelling/Word Choice.* List words marked as incorrectly spelled on your assignments. Master the words on your list and add new words as you accumulate assignments. Also include new, useful words with their brief definitions and comments on word choice, such as avoiding slang, clichés, and vague or general words.

- *Paragraph Development.* List suggestions your instructor made about writing strong topic sentences and attending to matters such as coherence, unity, emphasis, language, support, and sentences.

- *Grammar/Sentences.* As you go through this book, if you find that you did not completely master a section, list here any special problems you have before moving to the next section. Also, list comments from your instructor.

- *Punctuation/Capitalization.* List any problems you encounter with punctuation and capitalization. Because the items in this column may be covered in Chapter 10, you can often use both rule numbers and page numbers for the references here.

5. **Use the Writing Process Worksheet.** Record details about each of your assignments, such as the due date, topic, length, and form. The worksheet will also remind you of the stages of the writing process: explore, organize, and write. A blank Writing Process Worksheet for you to photocopy for assignments appears on page 202.

6. **Be positive.** All the elements you record in your Self-Evaluation Chart probably are covered in *At a Glance: Sentences.* The table of contents, the index, and the correction chart on the inside back cover of the book will direct you to the additional instruction you decide you need. Soon, seeing what you have mastered and checked off your list will give you a sense of accomplishment.

Finally, don't compare yourself with others. Compare yourself with yourself and, as you make progress, consider yourself what you are—a student on the path toward effective writing, a student on the path toward success.

✳ At a Glance

Sentences

※ **1**

Parts of Speech

To classify a word as a part of speech, we observe two simple principles:

- The word must be in the context of communication, usually in a sentence.
- We must be able to identify the word with others that have similar characteristics: nouns, pronouns, verbs, adjectives, adverbs, prepositions, conjunctions, or interjections. These are the eight parts of speech.

The first principle is important because some words can be any of several parts of speech. The word *round*, for example, can function as five:

- I watched the potter *round* the block of clay. (verb)
- I saw her go *round* the corner. (preposition)
- She has a *round* head. (adjective)
- The astronauts watched the world go *round*. (adverb)
- The champ knocked him out in one *round*. (noun)

※ Nouns

Nouns are naming words. Nouns may name persons, animals, plants, places, things, substances, qualities, or ideas—for example, *Bart, armadillo, Mayberry, tree, rock, cloud, love, ghost, music, virtue.*

Nouns are often pointed out by noun indicators. These noun indicators—*the, a, an*—signal that a noun is ahead, although there may be words between the indicator and the noun itself.

the slime	*a* werewolf	*an* aardvark
the green slime	*a* hungry werewolf	*an* angry aardvark

✳ Pronouns

A **pronoun** is a word that is used in place of a noun.

- Some pronouns may represent specific persons or things:

I	she	they	you
me	her	them	yourself
myself	herself	themselves	yourselves
it	he	we	who
itself	him	us	whom
that	himself	ourselves	

- Indefinite pronouns refer to nouns (persons, places, things) in a general way:

  each   everyone   nobody   somebody

- Other pronouns point out particular things:

  Singular   *this, that*   Plural   *these, those*

  This is my treasure.   *These* are my jewels.

  That is your junk.   *Those* are your trinkets.

- Still other pronouns introduce questions.

  Which is the best CD player?

  What are the main ingredients of a Twinkie?

✳ Verbs

Verbs show action or express being in relation to the subject of a sentence. They customarily occur in set positions in sentences.

- **Action verbs** are usually easy to identify.

  The aardvark *ate* the crisp, tasty ants. (action verb)

  The aardvark *washed* them down with a snoutful of water. (action verb)

- The ***being*** **verbs** are few in number and are also easy to identify. The most common *being* verbs are is, was, were, are, and am.

  Gilligan *is* on an island in the South Pacific. (*being* verb)

  I *am* his enthusiastic fan. (*being* verb)

- The form of a verb expresses its tense, that is, the time of the action or being. The time may be in the present or past.

    Roseanne *sings* "The Star-Spangled Banner." (present)

    Roseanne *sang* "The Star-Spangled Banner." (past)

- One or more **helping verbs** may be used with the main verb to form other tenses. The combination is called a **verb phrase**.

    She *had sung* the song many times in the shower. (Helping verb and main verb indicate a time in the past)

    She *will be singing* the song no more in San Diego. (Helping verbs and main verb indicate a time in the future)

- Some helping verbs can be used alone as main verbs: *has, have, had, is, was, were, are, am.* Certain other helping verbs function only as helpers: *will, shall, should, could.*

The most common position for the verb is directly after the subject or after the subject and its modifiers.

    At high noon only two men [subject] *were* on Main Street.

    The man with the faster draw [subject and modifiers] *walked* away alone.

☀ Adjectives

Adjectives modify nouns and pronouns. Most adjectives answer the questions *What kind? Which one?* and *How many?*

- Adjectives answering the *What kind?* question are descriptive. They tell the quality, kind, or condition of the nouns or pronouns they modify.

red convertible	*dirty* fork
noisy muffler	*wild* roses
The rain is *gentle.*	Bob was *tired.*

- Adjectives answering the *Which one?* question narrow or restrict the meaning of a noun. Some of these are pronouns that become adjectives by function.

my money	*our* ideas	the *other* house
this reason	*these* apples	

- Adjectives answering the *How many?* question are, of course, numbering words.

  some people   *each* pet   *few* goals
  three dollars   *one* glove

- The words *a, an,* and *the* are adjectives called **articles.** As "noun indicators," they point out persons, places, and things.

✳ Adverbs

Adverbs modify (describe or explain) verbs, adjectives, and other adverbs. Adverbs answer the questions *How? Where? When?* and *To what degree?*

<table>
<tr><td>Modifying verbs</td><td>They <u>did</u> their work <u>quickly</u>.
    v   adv</td></tr>
<tr><td></td><td>He <u>replied</u> <u>angrily</u>.
    v   adv</td></tr>
<tr><td>Modifying adjectives</td><td>They were <u>somewhat</u> <u>happy</u>.
         adv   adj</td></tr>
<tr><td>Modifying adverbs</td><td>He answered <u>very</u> <u>slowly</u>.
        adv   adv</td></tr>
</table>

- Adverbs that answer the *How?* question are concerned with manner or way.

  She ate the snails *hungrily.*   He snored *noisily.*

- Adverbs that answer the *Where?* question show location.

  They drove *downtown.*   She climbed *upstairs.*
  He stayed *behind.*

- Adverbs that answer the *When?* question indicate time.

  The ship sailed *yesterday.*   I expect an answer *soon.*

- Adverbs that answer the *To what degree?* question express extent.

  She is *entirely* correct.   He was *somewhat* annoyed.

Most words ending in *-ly* are adverbs.

  He completed the task <u>skillfully</u>.
                      adv

She answered him <u>courteously</u>.
                         adv

However, there are a few exceptions.

The house provided a <u>lovely</u> view of the valley.
                            adj

Your goblin mask is <u>ugly</u>.
                          adj

✳ Prepositions

A **preposition** is a word or words that function as a connective. The preposition connects its object(s) to some other word(s) in the sentence. A preposition and its object(s)—usually a noun or pronoun—with modifiers make up a **prepositional phrase.**

Bart worked <u>against</u> great <u>odds</u>.
            prep   object
            └──────┬──────┘
            prepositional phrase

Everyone <u>in</u> his <u>household</u> cheered his effort.
         prep   object
         └─────┬─────┘
         prepositional phrase

Following are some of the most common prepositions:

about	before	but	into	past
above	behind	by	like	to
across	below	despite	near	toward
after	beneath	down	of	under
against	beside	for	off	until
among	between	from	on	upon
around	beyond	in	over	with

Some prepositions are composed of more than one word and are formed from other parts of speech:

according to	as far as	because of	in spite of
ahead of	as well as	in back of	instead of
along with	aside from	in front of	together with

A prepositional phrase can serve as an adjective or adverb within the sentence structure.

The car <u>with</u> the <u>dent</u> is mine.
       prep   object

prepositional phrase modifying *car,* a noun
adjective

A storm is forming <u>on</u> the <u>horizon</u>.
           prep   object

prepositional phrase modifying *is forming,* a verb phrase
adverb

Caution: Do not confuse adverbs with prepositions

I went *across* slowly. (without an object—adverb)

I went *across* the field. (with an object—preposition)

We walked *behind* silently. (without an object—adverb)

We walked *behind* the mall. (with an object—preposition)

✳ Conjunctions

A **conjunction** connects and shows a relationship between words, phrases, or clauses. A phrase is two or more words acting as a part of speech. A clause is a group of words with a subject and a verb. An independent clause can stand by itself: *She plays bass guitar.* A dependent clause cannot stand by itself: *when she plays bass guitar.*

The two kinds of conjunctions are coordinating and subordinating.

Coordinating conjunctions connect words, phrases, and clauses of equal rank: noun with noun, adjective with adjective, verb with verb, phrase with phrase, main clause with main clause, and subordinate clause with subordinate clause. The seven common coordinating conjunctions are *for, and, nor, but, or, yet,* and *so.* (An easy way to remember them is to think of the acronym FANBOYS, which is made up of the first letter of each conjunction.)

Two nouns   Bring a <u>pencil</u> <u>and</u> some <u>paper</u>.
                   noun conj   noun

Two phrases   Did she go <u>to the store</u> <u>or</u> <u>to the game</u>?
                   prep phrase conj prep phrase

Paired conjunctions such as *either/or, neither/nor,* or *both/and* are usually classed as coordinating conjunctions.

<u>Neither</u> the coach <u>nor</u> the manager was at fault.
 conj   conj

Subordinating conjunctions connect dependent clauses with main clauses. Here is a list of the most common subordinating conjunctions:

after	because	provided	whenever
although	before	since	where
as	but that	so that	whereas
as if	if	till	wherever
as long as	in order that	until	
as soon as	notwithstanding	when	

If the dependent clause comes *before* the main clause, it is set off by a comma.

Although she was in pain, she stayed in the game.
    conj   sub   v
    └─────┬─────┘
      dependent clause

If the dependent clause comes *after* the main clause, it usually is *not* set off by a comma.

She stayed in the game because she was needed.
                          conj   sub   v
                          └─────┬──────┘
                            dependent clause

Caution: Certain words can function as either conjunctions or prepositions. It is necessary to look ahead to see if the word introduces a clause with a subject and verb—conjunction function—or takes an object—preposition function. Some of the words with two functions are *after, for, since,* and *until.*

After the concert was over, we went home. (clause follows—conjunction)

After the concert, we went home. (object follows—preposition)

✳ Interjections

An **interjection** conveys strong emotion or surprise. When an interjection appears alone, it is usually punctuated with an exclamation mark.

Wow!   Curses!   Cowabunga!   Yabba dabba doo!

When it appears as part of a sentence, an interjection is usually followed by a comma.

Oh, I did not consider that problem.

The interjection may sound exciting, but it is seldom appropriate for college writing.

✳ Chapter Review

Exercise 1 Identifying Parts of Speech

Identify the part of speech of each italicized word or group of words by placing the appropriate abbreviations in the blanks.

n	noun	pro	pronoun
v	verb	adj	adjective
adv	adverb	conj	conjunction
prep	preposition		

_____ _____   1. *For* about forty years, the Three Stooges were a popular *comedy* team.

_____ _____   2. They were *often* accused of making films *in* bad taste, but no one accused them of being good actors.

_____ _____   3. For decades they *made seven* or more pictures a year.

_____ _____   4. Actually six *different* actors *played* the parts.

_____ _____   5. The *most* famous threesome *was* Moe, Curley, and Larry.

_____ _____   6. The Stooges specialized *in physical* comedy.

_____ _____   7. They *took* special *delight* in hitting each other in the head and poking each other's eyes.

_____ _____   8. Moe was the on-screen *leader* of this *zany* group.

———— ———— 9. He assumed leadership in each film *because he* was more intelligent than the others, which isn't saying much.

———— ———— 10. Curley was not bright, but he made up for his *dumbness* by having the *hardest* head in the world, at least in the world of Stooge movies.

———— ———— 11. Larry *often got caught* between the flailing arms and kicking feet of Moe and Curley.

———— ———— 12. The movies made *by* the Stooges *usually* came in two reels and were shown along with feature-length films.

———— ———— 13. The Stooge movies *were given* such *titles* as *Half-Wits, Three Hams on Rye, Slap Happy Sleuths,* and *Matri Phony.*

———— ———— 14. They made fun of *dignity* and physically abused each other with all kinds *of* lethal instruments, but they never got hurt.

———— ———— 15. They received *little respect* from the film-making community.

———— ———— 16. Only Moe saved *his* money *and* became wealthy.

———— ———— 17. Apparently Curley *at* times lived his *movie* role off stage.

———— ———— 18. After a *brief* marriage, Curley's wife *left* him, saying he punched, poked, pinched, and pushed her and left cigar butts in the sink.

———— ———— 19. Moe tried to gain *respectability* as a character actor, but the audiences could never accept *him* in serious roles.

———— ———— 20. A whole new television *audience has made* the Three Stooges the stars they never were in their lifetimes.

Exercise 2 Identifying Parts of Speech

Identify the part of speech of each italicized word or group of words by placing the appropriate abbreviations in the blanks.

n	noun		pro	pronoun
v	verb		adj	adjective
adv	adverb		conj	conjunction
prep	preposition			

_____ _____ 1. *Before* gunpowder was invented, soldiers *often* wore armor.

_____ _____ 2. The armor *protected* the soldiers against *sharp* blows.

_____ _____ 3. Early armor was designed *from* layers of animal *hide*.

_____ _____ 4. The *first* designs were in the form *of* shields.

_____ _____ 5. Other designs *covered* the *entire* body.

_____ _____ 6. Whole battles were *sometimes* won or *lost* because of armor.

_____ _____ 7. *Armor* craftsmen had *important* positions in society.

_____ _____ 8. Chain mail *armor* was made *of* small connected rings.

_____ _____ 9. *Japanese* armor of the 1500s was made *of* thousands of fishlike scales.

_____ _____ 10. Most European armor was made of *large* metal plates shaped to the *body*.

_____ _____ 11. *Some* of it was designed with precious metals and decorated with *artistic* patterns.

——— ——— 12. The metal was *heavy, and* soldiers needed special assistance in mounting their horses.

——— ——— 13. Because the metal was *so* strong, knights *often* tried to unseat their opponents instead of trying to pierce the armor.

——— ——— 14. One famous soldier fell off his horse *and* into a stream *fifteen* inches deep.

——— ——— 15. His armor *filled* with water *and* he drowned.

——— ——— 16. *During* the crusades, European soldiers wore their *metal* armor into the deserts.

——— ——— 17. The *armor* often became so hot the soldiers fell off their horses *in* exhaustion.

——— ——— 18. With the development of the longbow *and* gunpowder, traditional armor *lost* its popularity.

——— ——— 19. Lightweight *armor* has been used in *modern* warfare.

——— ——— 20. The helmet is one *carryover* from earlier *designs*.

Subjects and Verbs

The two crucial parts of any sentence are the subject and the verb.

- The **subject** is who or what causes the action or expresses a state of being.
- The **verb** indicates what the subject is doing or is being.

The subject and verb often carry the meaning of the sentence. Consider this example:

> The <u>woman</u> <u>left</u> for work.
>   subject   verb

The subject *woman* and the verb *left* indicate the basic content of the sentence while providing structure. So important are the subject and the verb that they alone are sufficient to create a complete sentence.

> He runs.
>
> She thinks.

✳ Subjects

The **simple subject** of a sentence is usually a single noun or pronoun.

> The judge's <u>reputation</u> for order in the courtroom is well known.
>   simple subject

The **complete subject** is the simple subject with all its modifiers—that is, with all the words that describe or qualify it.

> <u>The judge's reputation for order in the courtroom</u> is well known.
>   complete subject

To more easily identify simple subjects of sentences, you may want to review the following information about nouns and pronouns. (You may also review Chapter 1, "Parts of Speech.")

Nouns

Nouns are naming words. Nouns may name persons, animals, plants, places, things, substances, qualities, or ideas—for example, *Bart, armadillo, Mayberry, tree, rock, cloud, love, ghost, music,* and *virtue.*

Pronouns

A **pronoun** is a word that is used in place of a noun.

- Pronouns that can be used as subjects of sentences may represent specific persons or things and are called personal pronouns:

I	we
you	you
he, she, it	they

  EXAMPLE   <u>They</u> recommended my sister for the coaching position.
  subject

- Indefinite pronouns refer to nouns (persons, places, things) in a general way:

each	everyone	nobody	somebody
either	neither	anyone	someone

  EXAMPLE   <u>Everyone</u> wants a copy of that photograph.
  subject

- Other pronouns point out particular things:

  SINGULAR *this, that*   PLURAL *these, those*

  This is my treasure.   *These* are my jewels.

  That is your junk.   *Those* are your trinkets.

- Still other pronouns introduce questions:

  Which is the best CD player?

  What are the main ingredients in a Twinkie?

  Who understands this computer command?

Caution: To be the subject of a sentence, a pronoun must stand alone.

  This is a treasure. (Subject is *this*; pronoun stands alone.)

  This *treasure* is mine. (Subject is *treasure*. *This* is an adjective—a word that describes a noun; *this* describes *treasure*.)

Compound Subjects

A subject may be **compound.** That is, it may consist of two or more subjects, usually joined by *and* or *or,* that function together.

> The *prosecutor* and the *attorney* for the defense made opening statements.

> *He* and his *friends* listened carefully.

Implied Subjects

A subject may be **implied** or understood. An imperative sentence— a sentence that gives a command—has *you* as the implied subject.

> (You) Sit in that chair, please.

> (You) Now take the oath.

> (You) Please read the notes carefully.

Trouble Spots

A **prepositional phrase** starts with a preposition (a word like *at, in, of, to, with*) and ends with one or more nouns or pronouns with their modifiers: *at the time, by the jury, in the courtroom, to the judge and the media, with controlled anger.* Some of the most common prepositions are the following:

about	before	but	into	past
above	behind	by	like	to
across	below	despite	near	toward
after	beneath	down	of	under
against	beside	for	off	until
among	between	from	on	upon
around	beyond	in	over	with

Some prepositions are composed of more than one word and are formed from other parts of speech:

according to	as far as	because of	in spite of
ahead of	as well as	in back of	instead of
along with	aside from	in front of	together with

Be careful not to confuse the subject of a sentence with the noun or pronoun (known as the **object of the preposition**) in a prepositional phrase. The object of a preposition (the final noun or pronoun of a prepositional phrase) cannot be the subject of a sentence.

> The <u>car</u> <u>with the dents</u> is mine.
> subject/prepositional phrase

The subject of the sentence is *car*. The word *dents* is the object of the preposition *with* and cannot be the subject of the sentence.

> <u>Most</u> <u>of the pie</u> has been eaten.
> subject/prepositional phrase

> The <u>person</u> <u>in the middle</u> <u>of the crowd</u> has disappeared.
> subject/prepositional phrase/prepositional phrase

The words *there* and *here* are adverbs (or filler words) and cannot be subjects.

> There is no <u>problem.</u>
> subject

> Here is the <u>issue.</u>
> subject

Exercise 1 Finding Subjects

Underline the simple or the compound subject, without modifiers.

EXAMPLE A highly developed social <u>structure</u> and the <u>use</u> of bronze were marks of the Shang dynasty (about 1766 to 1122 B.C.).

1. The earliest evidence of Chinese writing comes from that

   dynasty.

2. Archaeologists have found hundreds of animal bones and shells.

3. The bones and shells have written symbols on them.

4. These objects with writing on them are known as oracle bones.

5. Priests told fortunes with them.

6. Part of today's Chinese culture was developed 3,500 years ago.

7. In the Chinese method of writing, each character stands for an idea, not for a sound.

8. Some of the characters are very much like those in a modern Chinese newspaper.

9. They are not like Egyptian hieroglyphs.

10. Those Egyptian symbols stood for sounds in the spoken language.

11. In the Chinese language, there are practically no links between written and spoken forms.

12. Study your Chinese 101 textbook for more insights.

Exercise 2 Finding Subjects

Underline the simple or the compound subject, without modifiers.

1. Mahatma Gandhi gave his life for India and for peace.

2. Through a practice of nonviolent resistance, he led his people to freedom from the British.

3. Ponder his preference for behavior rather than accomplishment.

4. There was only good in his behavior and in his accomplishments.

5. His fasts, writings, and speeches inspired the people of India.

6. He taught his people self-sufficiency in weaving cloth and making salt for themselves against British law.

7. Gandhi urged the tolerance of all religions.

8. Finally, the British granted freedom to India.

9. Some leaders in India and a few foreign agitators questioned

   the freedom of religion.

10. Gandhi, the Indian prince of peace, was killed by an intolerant

    religious leader.

✳ Verbs

Verbs show action or express being in relation to the subject of a sentence.

Types of Verbs

Action verbs show movement or accomplishment of an idea or a deed. Someone can "*consider* the statement" or "*hit* the ball." Here are other examples:

> She *left* the arena.
> He *bought* the book.
> They *adopted* the child.
> He *understood* her main theories.

Being verbs indicate existence. Few in number, they include *is, was, were, am,* and *are.*

> The movie *is* sad.
> The book *was* comprehensive.
> They *were* responsible.
> I *am* concerned.
> We *are* organized.

Verb Phrases

Verbs may occur as single words or as phrases. A **verb phrase** is made up of a main verb and one or more helping verbs such as the following:

is	was	can	have
are	were	could	had
am	will	would	has

Here are some sentences that contain verb phrases:

The judge *has presided* over many capital cases.

His rulings *are* seldom *overturned* on appeal.

I *should have known* the answer.

Compound Verbs

Verbs that are joined by a word such as *and* or *or* are called **compound verbs.**

The prosecutor *had presented* and *had won* famous cases.

She *prepared* carefully and *presented* her ideas with clarity.

We *will go* out for dinner or *skip* it entirely.

Compound verbs show two physical or mental actions performed by a simple or a compound subject.

Verbals

Do not confuse verbs with verbals. **Verbals** are verblike words in certain respects, but they function as other parts of speech. The three kinds of verbals are infinitives, gerunds, and participles.

An **infinitive** is made up of the word *to* and a verb. An infinitive provides information, but unlike the true verb it is not tied to the subject of the sentence. It acts as a noun or describing unit.

He wanted *to get* a bachelor's degree. (As an object of the verb *wanted, to get* acts as a noun and is an infinitive.)

A bachelor's degree is not easy *to obtain.* (As a modifier, or describer, of *easy, to obtain* acts as an adverb and is an infinitive.)

A **gerund** is a verblike word ending in *-ing* that acts as a noun.

Going to work was her main objective. (the activity of going to work)

She thought about *going* to work. (the act of going)

Going in each sentence acts as a noun. In the first sentence, it is the subject of the sentence. In the second, it is the object of the preposition *about.*

A **participle** is a verblike word that usually has an *-ing* or an *-ed* ending.

> *Walking* to town in the dark, he lost his way.

> *Wanted* by the FBI, she was on the run.

In the first example, the word *walking* answers the question *when?* In the second, the word *wanted* answers the question *which one?* Both *walking* and *wanted* are describing words; they are not the true verbs in the sentences.

Caution: Do not confuse verbals with true verbs. Verbals serve as nouns or modifiers. *Never, not,* and *hardly* are also modifiers, not verbs.

> The attorney could *not* win the case without key witnesses. (*Not* is an adverb. The verb phrase is *could win.*)

> The jury could *hardly* hear the witness. (*Hardly* is an adverb; *could hear* is the verb phrase.)

Exercise 3   Finding Verbs

Underline the verb(s) in each sentence.

1. Chimpanzees live and travel in social groups.

2. The composition of these groups varies in age and gender.

3. The habitat of the chimpanzees is mainly forests.

4. They spend more time in the trees than on the ground.

5. Each night they make a nest of branches and leaves in trees.

6. Sometimes a proud male will beat on his chest.

7. Chimpanzees are violent at times but usually live peacefully.

8. After finding food, a chimp hoots and shakes branches.

9. Other chimps hear the commotion and go to the food source.

10. Chimp tools, such as leaf sponges and sticks, are primitive.

Exercise 4 Finding Verbs

Underline the verb(s) in each sentence.

1. Chimpanzees share many features with human beings.

2. More than 90 percent of basic genetic make-up is shared.

3. Both human beings and chimps can use reason.

4. Chimps have a remarkable talent for communication.

5. Chimps do not have the capacity for human speech.

6. However, chimps can use other symbols.

7. In one experiment, chimps learned American Sign Language.

8. Chimps can learn a complex system of language.

9. Chimp scholar Washoe has learned more than 160 signs and can ask questions.

10. Another chimp, Lana, uses a computer.

Exercise 5 Finding Subjects and Verbs

Circle the subject(s) and underline the verb(s) in the following sentences. You will have to supply the subject for one sentence.

1. Read this exercise carefully.

2. What causes earthquakes?

3. How much damage can they do?

4. Earthquakes shake the earth.

5. There is no simple answer to the question of cause.

6. The earth is covered by rock plates.

7. Instead of merely covering, they are in constant motion.

8. These plates bump into each other and then pass over each other.

9. The rocks are squeezed and stretched.

10. They pull apart or pile up and cause breaks in the earth's surface.

11. These breaks are called *faults*.

12. The formation of a fault is an earthquake.

13. During the breaking or shifting, a seismic wave travels across the earth's surface.

14. These quaking vibrations are especially destructive near the point of the breaking or shifting.

15. Their force is equal to as much as ten thousand times that of an atomic bomb.

16. For many years, scientists have tried to predict earthquakes.

17. There has been little success in their endeavors.

18. Earthquakes are identified only after the fact.

19. Some states, such as California, experience many earthquakes.

20. Somewhere in the earth, a quake of some magnitude is almost certainly occurring now.

✳ Location of Subjects and Verbs

Although the subject *usually* appears before the verb, it may follow
the verb instead:

> Into the court <u>stumbled</u> the <u>defendant</u>.
>   verb   subject

> From tiny acorns <u>grow</u> mighty <u>oaks</u>.
>   verb   subject

> There <u>was</u> little <u>support</u> for him in the audience.
>   verb   subject

> Here <u>are</u> your <u>books</u> and your <u>papers</u>.
>   verb   subject   subject

Verb phrases are often broken up in a question. Do not overlook
a part of the verb that is separated from another in a question such as
"Where had the defendant gone on that fateful night?" If you have
trouble finding the verb phrase, recast the question, making it into a
statement: "The defendant *had gone* where on that fateful night."
The result will not necessarily be a smooth or complete statement,
but you will be able to see the basic elements more easily.

> Can the defense lawyer control the direction of the trial?

Change the question to a statement to find the verb phrase:

> The defense lawyer *can control* the direction of the trial.

✳ Chapter Review

Exercise 6 Finding Subjects and Verbs

*Circle the subject(s) and underline the verb(s) in the following
sentences. You will have to supply the subject for one sentence.*

1. Consider this information about Puerto Rico.

2. Just where is Puerto Rico?

3. What do the words *Puerto Rico* mean?

4. Are Puerto Ricans U.S. citizens?

5. How is Puerto Rico different from our states?

6. Will it ever become a state?

7. The Commonwealth of Puerto Rico is located southeast of Florida.

8. *Puerto Rico* means "rich port."

9. Puerto Rico became a U.S. territory in 1898 after the Spanish-American War.

10. It became a commonwealth with its own constitution in 1952.

11. Puerto Ricans are citizens of the United States.

12. They cannot vote in presidential elections and do not pay federal income taxes.

13. On several occasions, they have voted not to become a state.

14. However, there are many in favor of statehood.

15. The majority of the citizens speak Spanish.

16. Their economy is based on manufacturing, fishing, and agriculture.

17. The Caribbean National Forest is treasured by Puerto Ricans and visitors.

18. In this tropical rain forest, parrots and orchids can be seen.

19. Tourists by the thousands visit the Phosphorescent Bay at La Parguera.

20. On moonless nights, the phosphorescent plankton light the water.

Exercise 7 Finding Subjects and Verbs

Circle the simple or the compound subject(s) and underline the verb(s) in the following sentences. You will have to supply the subject for one sentence.

1. Read this exercise and learn about the Aztec empire in Mexico.

2. Aztec cities were as large as those in Europe at that time.

3. Government and religion were important concerns.

4. There was little difference between the two institutions.

5. They built huge temples to their gods and sacrificed human beings.

6. The religious ceremonies related mainly to their concerns about plentiful harvests.

7. Aztec society had nobles, commoners, serfs, and slaves.

8. The family included a husband, a wife, children, and some relatives of the husband.

9. At the age of ten, boys went to school, and girls either went to school or learned domestic skills at home.

10. The Aztecs wore loose-fitting garments, they lived in adobe houses, and they ate tortillas.

11. Scholars in this culture developed a calendar of 365 days.

12. Huge Aztec calendars of stone are now in museums.

13. The Aztec language was similar to that of the Comanche and Pima Indians.

14. The Aztec written language was pictographic and represented ideas and sounds.

15. Both religion and government required young men to pursue
    warfare.

16. By pursuing warfare, the soldiers could capture others for
    slaves and sacrifice, and enlarge the Aztec empire.

17. In 1519, Hernando Cortez landed in Mexico.

18. He was joined by Indians other than Aztecs.

19. After first welcoming Cortez and his army, the Aztecs then
    rebelled.

20. The Spaniards killed Emperor Montezuma II, and then they
    defeated the Aztecs.

Exercise 8 Writing Sentences with Subjects and Verbs

Using the topic of work, *write five sentences. Circle the simple or
the compound subject(s) and underline the verb(s).*

1. _____

   _____

   _____

   _____

   _____

2. _____

   _____

   _____

3. _____

4. _____

5. _____

✳ 3

Kinds of Sentences

The four kinds of basic sentences in English are simple, compound, complex, and compound-complex. The terms may be new to you, but if you can recognize subjects and verbs, with a little instruction and practice you should be able to identify and write any of the four kinds of sentences. The only new idea to master is the concept of the *clause.*

✳ Clauses

A **clause** is a group of words with a subject and a verb that functions as a part or all of a complete sentence. There are two kinds of clauses: independent (main) and dependent (subordinate).

INDEPENDENT CLAUSE   I have the money.

DEPENDENT CLAUSE   When I have the money

Independent Clauses

An **independent (main) clause** is a group of words with a subject and a verb that can stand alone and make sense. An independent clause expresses a complete thought by itself and can be written as a separate sentence.

She plays the bass guitar.

The manager is not at fault.

Dependent Clauses

A **dependent clause** is a group of words with a subject and a verb that depends on a main clause to give it meaning.

since Helen came home (no meaning alone)

<u>Since Helen came home,</u> <u>her mother has been happy.</u> (has meaning)
    dependent clause   independent clause

because she was needed (no meaning alone)

<u>She stayed in the game</u> <u>because she was needed.</u> (has meaning)
    independent clause   dependent clause

Dependent clauses are connected to the rest of the sentence by subordinating conjunctions such as the following:

after	if	until
although	in order that	when
as	provided that	whenever
as if	rather than	where
because	since	whereas
before	so that	wherever
even if	than	whether
even though	unless	while

Relative Clauses

A **relative clause,** one type of dependent clause, begins with a relative pronoun, a pronoun like *that, which,* or *who.* Relative pronouns *relate* the clause to another word in the sentence.

that fell last night (no meaning alone)

The snow <u>that fell last night</u> is nearly gone. (has meaning)
        dependent clause

In the sentence above, the relative pronoun *that* relates the dependent clause to the subject of the sentence, *snow.*

who stayed in the game (no meaning alone)

<u>She was the only one</u> <u>who stayed in the game.</u>
    independent clause   dependent clause

In the sentence above, the relative pronoun *who* relates the dependent clause to the word *one.*

Trouble Spot: Phrases

A **phrase** is a group of words that go together. It differs from a clause in that a phrase does not have a subject and a verb. So far, we have seen prepositional phrases (*in the house, beyond the horizon*) and verbal phrases (infinitive phrase: *to go home*; participial phrase: *disconnected from the printer*; and gerund phrase: *running the computer*).

Exercise 1 Identifying Clauses and Phrases

Identify the following groups of words as an independent, or main, clause (has a subject and verb and can stand alone); a dependent clause (has a subject and verb but cannot stand alone); or a phrase (a group of words that go together but do not have a subject and verb).

_____	1. Under the table
_____	2. After I baked the apple pie
_____	3. I baked an apple pie.
_____	4. To find a fossil
_____	5. Mr. Jones found a fossil.
_____	6. Over the bridge and through the woods
_____	7. We chased the wind over the bridge and through the woods.
_____	8. Which is on the floor
_____	9. Find your new socks.
_____	10. Because of the new guidelines
_____	11. Standing on the corner
_____	12. Why are we standing on the corner?

✳ Types of Sentences

The following discussion covers sentence types according to this principle: On the basis of the number and kinds of clauses it contains, a sentence may be classified as simple, compound, complex, or compound-complex.

Type	Definition	Example
Simple	One independent clause	She did the work well.
Compound	Two or more independent clauses	She did the work well, and she was paid well.
Complex	One independent clause and one or more dependent clauses	*Because she did the work well,* she was paid well.
Compound-Complex	Two or more independent clauses and one or more dependent clauses	*Because she did the work well,* she was paid well, and she was satisfied.

Simple Sentences

A **simple sentence** consists of one independent clause and no dependent clauses. It may contain phrases and have more than one subject or verb.

> The *lake looks* beautiful in the moonlight. (one subject and one verb)

> The *Army, Navy,* and *Marines sent* troops to the disaster area. (three subjects and one verb)

> *We sang* the old songs and *danced* happily at their wedding. (one subject and two verbs)

> My *father, mother,* and *sister came* to the school play, *applauded* the performers, and *attended* the party afterwards. (three subjects and three verbs)

Exercise 2 Writing Simple Sentences

Write six simple sentences. The first five have been started for you.

1. This school _____

   _____

2. My desk _____

   _____

3. My friend _____

   _____

4. In the evening, I _____

_____

5. Last night, the _____

_____

6. _____

_____

Compound Sentences

A **compound sentence** consists of two or more independent clauses with no dependent clauses. Take, for example, the following two independent clauses:

> He opened the door. He found the missing paper.

Here are three ways to join the independent clauses to form a compound sentence.

1. Connect the two independent clauses using a connecting word called a **coordinating conjunction.** The coordinating conjunctions are *for, and, nor, but, or, yet, so.* Remember the acronym FANBOYS.

   > He opened the door, *and* he found the missing paper.

   > He opened the door, *so* he found the missing paper.

   Use a comma before the coordinating conjunction between two independent clauses (unless one of the clauses is extremely short).

2. Put a semicolon between the clauses.

   > He opened the door; he found the missing paper.

3. Use a transitional word, such as *however* or *therefore.* Place a semicolon before the word and a comma after.

   > He found the missing paper; *therefore,* he was satisfied.

Exercise 3 Writing Compound Sentences

Write five compound sentences using coordinating conjunctions. The sentences have been started for you. Then write the same five compound sentences without the coordinating conjunctions. Use a semicolon to join the independent clauses, and, if appropriate, in-clude transitional words such as therefore *and* however.

1. He played well in the first quarter, but he _____

   _____

2. She was happy for a while, and then _____

3. The dog is our best friend, for _____

   _____

4. She is not the best player, nor is _____

   _____

5. I will try to help, but _____

   _____

6. _____

   _____

7. _____

   _____

8. _____

   _____

9. _____

   _____

10. _____

   _____

Complex Sentences

A **complex sentence** consists of one independent clause and one or more dependent clauses. In the following sentences, the dependent clauses are italicized.

> *When lilacs are in bloom,* we love to visit friends in the country. (one dependent clause and one independent clause)
>
> *Although it rained last night,* we decided to take the path *that led through the woods.* (one independent clause and two dependent clauses)

A relative clause (see page 28) can be the dependent clause in a complex sentence.

> I knew the actress *who played that part in the 1980s.*

Punctuation tip: Use a comma after a dependent clause that appears before the main clause.

> *When the bus arrived,* we quickly boarded.

Exercise 4 Writing Complex Sentences

Write six complex sentences. The first five have been started for you.

1. Although he did the work quickly, _____

_____

2. _____

because the storm hit.

3. After you go to the party, _____

_____

4. Because you are smart, _____

_____

5. _____

_____ when he turned to leave.

6. _____

_____

Compound-Complex Sentences

A **compound-complex sentence** consists of two or more independent clauses and one or more dependent clauses.

> Albert enlisted in the Army, and Robert, who was his older brother, joined him a day later.

INDEPENDENT	
CLAUSES	Albert enlisted in the Army
	Robert joined him a day later

DEPENDENT CLAUSE	who was his older brother
	Because Mr. Roberts was a talented teacher, he was voted teacher of the year, and his students prospered.
INDEPENDENT CLAUSES	he was voted teacher of the year his students prospered
DEPENDENT CLAUSE	Because Mr. Roberts was a talented teacher

Exercise 5 Writing Compound-Complex Sentences

Write six compound-complex sentences. The first five have been started for you.

1. Because he was my friend, I had to defend him, and I _____

   _____

2. Although he started late, he finished rapidly, and he _____

   _____

3. She had not eaten since the clock struck twelve, and she _____

   _____

4. We didn't realize that he was sick, but _____

   _____

5. If you want to leave, _____

   _____

6. _____

   _____

✳ Chapter Review

Exercise 6 Identifying Types of Sentences

Label each sentence as simple, compound, complex, or compound-complex.

_____ 1. Most hummingbirds weigh less than a nickel.

_____ 2. Because they're so tiny, people think of them as cute, sweet little birds.

_____ 3. However, hummingbirds are very mean, and they have been dubbed the "junkyard dogs" of the bird world.

_____ 4. A male hummingbird will fiercely guard a nectar feeder or a patch of flowers, and if any other hummingbirds come near, he will attack them.

_____ 5. The bird will threaten intruders, chase them, ram them in mid-air, and try to stab them with its beak.

_____ 6. Hummingbirds can even intimidate birds like hawks, which are a hundred times their size.

_____ 7. These territorial birds can be vicious, but they do have a good reason.

_____ 8. They expend a lot of energy; as a matter of fact, their hearts beat 1,200 times a minute, and their wings beat at over 2,000 revolutions per minute.

_____ 9. To survive, a hummingbird must consume 7 to 12 calories per day; in human terms, that would be 204,300 calories per day, which is the amount in 171 pounds of hamburger.

_____ 10. If you had to round up that much grub every day, you, too, might get very protective of your food source.

Combining Sentences

The simple sentence, the most basic sentence in the English language, can be exceptionally useful and powerful. Some of the greatest statements in literature have been presented in the simple sentence. Its strength is in its singleness of purpose. However, a piece of writing made up of a long series of simple sentences is likely to be monotonous. Moreover, the form may suggest a separateness of ideas that does not serve your purpose well. If your ideas are closely related, some equal in importance and some not, you can combine sentences to show the relationships between your ideas.

※ Coordination: The Compound Sentence

If you intend to communicate two equally important and closely related ideas, you certainly will want to place them close together, probably in a compound sentence.

Suppose we take two simple sentences that we want to combine:

I am very tired. I worked very hard today.

We have already looked at coordinating conjunctions as a way of joining independent clauses to create compound sentences. Depending on which coordinating conjunction you use, you can show different kinds of relationships. (The following list is arranged according to the FANBOYS acronym. Only the first conjunction joins the original two sentences.)

For shows a reason:
I am very tired, *for* I worked very hard today.

And shows equal ideas:
I am very tired, *and* I want to rest for a few minutes.

Nor indicates a negative choice or alternative:
I am not tired, *nor* am I hungry right now.

But shows contrast:
I am very tired, *but* I have no time to rest now.

Or indicates a choice or an alternative:
I will take a nap, *or* I will go out jogging.

Yet indicates contrast:
I am very tired, *yet* I am unable to relax.

So points to a result:
I am very tired, *so* I will take a nap.

Punctuation with Coordinating Conjunctions

When you combine two sentences by using a coordinating conjunction, drop the period, change the capital letter to a small letter, and insert a comma before the coordinating conjunction.

$$
\text{Independent clause}
\left\{
\begin{array}{l}
, for \\
, and \\
, nor \\
, but \\
, or \\
, yet \\
, so
\end{array}
\right\}
\text{independent clause.}
$$

Exercise 1 Combining Sentences: Compound

Combine the following pairs of sentences by deleting the first period, changing the capital letter that begins the second sentence to a small letter, and inserting a comma and an appropriate coordinating conjunction from the FANBOYS list. Feel free to reword the sentences as necessary.

1. James Francis "Jim" Thorpe, a Sac and Fox Indian, was born in 1888 near Prague, Oklahoma. At the age of sixteen, he left home to enroll in the Carlisle Indian School in Pennsylvania.

2. He had had little experience playing football. He led his small college to victories against championship teams.

3. He had scarcely heard of other sports. He golfed in the 70s, bowled above 200, and played varsity basketball and lacrosse.

4. In the 1912 Olympic Games for amateur athletes at
   Stockholm, Jim Thorpe entered the two most rigorous events,
   the decathlon and the pentathlon. He won both.

5. King Gustav V of Sweden told him, "You, Sir, are the greatest
   athlete in the world." Jim Thorpe said, "Thanks, King."

6. Later it was said he had once been paid fifteen dollars a week to
   play baseball, making him a professional athlete. The Olympic
   medals were taken from him.

7. Soon a Major League baseball scout did offer Thorpe a respectable
   contract. He played in the National League for six seasons.

8. Not content to play only one sport, he also earned a good salary
   for that time in professional football. After competing for
   fifteen years, he said he had never played for the money.

9. Many regard Jim Thorpe as the greatest athlete of the
   twentieth century. He excelled in many sports at the highest
   levels of athletic competition.

10. Off the playing fields, he was known by his friends as a modest,
    quiet man. On the fields, he was a person of joyful combat.

Semicolons and Conjunctive Adverbs

We have also already looked at using a semicolon to join independent clauses to make a compound sentence. Here are two more simple sentences to combine:

> We were late. We missed the first act.

We can make one compound sentence out of them by joining the two clauses with a semicolon:

> We were late; we missed the first act.

We can also use words called conjunctive adverbs after semicolons to make the relationship between the two clauses clearer. Look at how the conjunctive adverb *therefore* adds the idea of "as a result."

> We were late; *therefore,* we missed the first act.

Conjunctive adverbs include the following words and phrases: *also, consequently, furthermore, hence, however, in fact, moreover, nevertheless, now, on the other hand, otherwise, soon, therefore, similarly, then, thus.*

When you coordinate ideas with conjunctive adverbs, consider the meanings of these words:

> As a result of: *therefore, consequently, hence, thus, then*
> To the contrary or with reservation: *however, nevertheless, otherwise, on the other hand*
> In addition to: *moreover, also*
> To emphasize or specify: *in fact, for example*
> To compare: *similarly*

Punctuation with Semicolons and Conjunctive Adverbs

When you combine two sentences by using a semicolon, replace the period with a semicolon and change the capital letter that begins the second sentence to a small letter. If you wish to use a conjunctive adverb, insert it after the semicolon and usually put a comma after it. (However, usually no comma follows *then, now, thus,* and *soon.*) The first letters of ten common conjunctive adverbs make up the acronym HOTSHOT CAT.

$$
\text{Independent clause} \left\{ \begin{array}{l} \text{; } \textit{however,} \\ \text{; } \textit{otherwise,} \\ \text{; } \textit{therefore,} \\ \text{; } \textit{similarly,} \\ \text{; } \textit{hence} \\ \text{; } \textit{on the other hand,} \\ \text{; } \textit{then} \\ \text{; } \textit{consequently,} \\ \text{; } \textit{also,} \\ \text{; } \textit{thus} \end{array} \right\} \text{independent clause.}
$$

Exercise 2   Combining Sentences: Compound

Combine each of the following pairs of sentences by replacing the first period with a semicolon, changing the capital letter that begins the second sentence to a small letter, and inserting a conjunctive adverb if appropriate. Consider the list of conjunctive adverbs (HOTSHOT CAT and others). Do not use a conjunctive adverb in every sentence.

1. Camels can cover much distance in heat with little or no water. They are well adapted to the desert.

2. They can walk easily on soft sand and carry heavy loads. They are useful pack animals for human beings traveling in the desert.

3. The typical desert offers little vegetation. That circumstance does not affect the camel.

4. A camel stores food in one or two humps of fat on its back. When food is scarce, the camel uses that fat for energy.

5. The Arabian camel has one hump. The Bactrian has two.

6. Camels are known for their bad temper. Most people are not surprised when camels bite, kick, and spit.

7. Camels grunt and groan when mounted. Once under way, they carry their loads patiently.

8. Camels have mouth linings as tough as leather. They can eat a thorny cactus without injuring themselves.

9. In the 1850s, the U.S. Army imported camels for desert transportation. The development of the railroads made camels unnecessary.

10. Working camels in Africa live for as long as fifty years. In

    circuses and zoos they die by the age of thirty.

✳ Subordination: The Complex Sentence

Whereas a compound sentence contains independent clauses that are equally important and closely related, a complex sentence combines ideas of unequal value. The following two sentences can be combined as either a compound sentence or a complex sentence, depending on whether the writer thinks the ideas are of equal value.

My neighbors are considerate. They never play loud music.

Combined as a compound sentence, suggesting that the ideas are of equal value, the new sentence looks like this:

<u>My neighbors are considerate</u>, and <u>they never play loud music.</u>

| independent clause | independent clause |
| (main idea) | (main idea) |

Here are the same two ideas combined as a complex sentence, suggesting that the ideas are of unequal value:

<u>Because my neighbors are considerate,</u> <u>they never play loud music.</u>

| dependent clause | independent clause |
| (less important idea) | (main idea) |

Although both the compound and complex forms are correct, the complex form conveys the ideas more precisely in this sentence because one idea does seem to be more important—one idea depends on the other.

Thus if you have two sentences with closely related ideas and one is clearly more important than the other, consider combining them in a complex sentence. Compare these two paragraphs:

- Version 1 contains six simple sentences, implying that the ideas are of equal value:

  (1) I was very upset. (2) The Fourth of July fireworks were especially loud. (3) My dog ran away. (4) The animal control officer made his morning rounds. (5) He found my dog in another part of town. (6) I was relieved.

- Version 2 consists of two simple sentences and two complex sentences, showing that some ideas are more important than others:

(1) I was very upset. (2) Because the Fourth of July fireworks were especially loud, my dog ran away. (3) When the animal control officer made his morning rounds, he found my dog in another part of town. (4) I was relieved.

You will probably consider Version 2 superior to Version 1. Sentences 2 and 3 are closely related, but 3 is more important. And sentences 4 and 5 are closely related, but 5 is more important. The revision made each pair into a complex sentence.

Although you could combine sentences 1 and 2, the result would be illogical because the wrong idea would be conveyed:

I was very upset because the Fourth of July fireworks were especially loud.

The person was very upset because the dog ran away, not because the fireworks were especially loud.

As you learned in Chapter 3, a complex sentence is composed of one independent clause and one or more dependent clauses. In combining two independent clauses to write a complex sentence, your first step is to decide on a word that will best show the relationship between the clauses. Words that show the relationship of a dependent clause to an independent one are called subordinating conjunctions. The italicized words in the sentences that follow are subordinating conjunctions. Consider the meaning as well as the placement of each one.

Because the storm hit, the game was canceled.

After the storm passed, the clown dogs began to bark.

When she read her poem, they were moved to fits of hysterics.

He did not volunteer to work on the holiday, *although* the pay was good.

No one has visited her *since* she moved into town.

They decided to wait *until* the cows came home.

They refused to work *unless* they were allowed to wear chef's hats.

Before the session ended, all the "hep cats" blew some sweet sounds.

Other subordinating conjunctions include the following:

as	even if	if	provided that
as if	even though	in order that	rather than

| so that | whenever | whereas | whether |
| than | where | wherever | while |

Punctuation with Subordinating Conjunctions

If the dependent clause comes *before* the main clause, set it off with a comma.

> Before you dive, be sure there is water in the pool.

If the dependent clause comes *after* or *within* the main clause, set it off only if the clause is not necessary to the meaning of the main clause or if the dependent clause begins with the word *although* or *though*.

> Be sure there is water in the pool *before* you dive.
>
> We went home *after* the concert had ended.
>
> He continued, *although* he had painted the cabinet twice.

You have already learned that a relative clause—one that starts with a relative pronoun like *that*, *which*, or *who*—can be the dependent clause in a sentence. If we look at the two sentences we started with, we can see how they can be combined using a relative clause.

> My neighbors are considerate. They never play loud music.

Combined as a complex sentence with a relative clause as the dependent clause, the new sentence looks like this:

> My neighbors, <u>who are considerate,</u> never play loud music.
>   dependent clause

Punctuation with Relative Pronouns

Set the dependent clause off with commas when it is not necessary to the sentence. Do not set the clause off if it is necessary for the meaning of the sentence.

> Everyone *who tries* will pass this class. (The dependent clause is necessary because one would not say, "Everyone will pass this class.")
>
> John, *who tries*, will pass this class. (The dependent clause is not necessary because one can say, "John will pass this class.")

The relative pronoun *which* usually refers to things. The word *which* almost always indicates that a clause is not necessary for the meaning of the sentence. Therefore, a clause beginning with *which* is almost always set off by commas.

> My car, *which is ten years old*, has a flat tire.

The relative pronoun *that* also usually refers to things. However, the word *that* almost always indicates that the clause *is* necessary for the meaning of the sentence. Therefore, a clause beginning with *that* is *not* set off by commas.

> The car *that* has a flat tire is ten years old.

The relative pronouns *who* and *whom*, as well as *whoever* and *whomever*, usually refer to people. Clauses that begin with those relative pronouns are not set off by commas if they are necessary for the meaning of the sentence; if they are not necessary, they are set off.

> A person *who* has a way with words is often quoted. (necessary for the meaning of the sentence)
>
> My uncle, *whom* I quote often, has a way with words. (not necessary for the meaning of the sentence)

Exercise 3 Combining Sentences: Complex

Combine each of the following pairs of sentences into one complex sentence. Change the capital letter to a small letter when necessary, delete the period, insert an appropriate subordinating conjunction or relative pronoun, add necessary punctuation, and make other minor changes as needed.

1. Mary Hayes was one of the first female soldiers in American

   warfare. She is better known as Molly Pitcher.

2. At the outbreak of the War of Independence, Mary was the wife

   of John Hayes. He soon joined the army.

3. Following established practice, Mary Hayes also went to war.

   She was the wife of a soldier.

4. He performed military duties. She washed and mended clothes

   and cooked meals.

5. John Hayes' regiment fought at the Battle of Monmouth. The day was hot.

6. Mary Hayes brought the soldiers water in pitchers. Some men started calling her Molly Pitcher, "Molly" for "Mary" and "Pitcher" for what she carried.

7. She was immediately proud of the name. Others started using it.

8. John Hayes suffered a heat stroke. Mary Hayes took over his job, firing his cannon.

9. A cannonball sailed between her knees and tore her dress. She refused to stop fighting.

10. Following the war, Mary Hayes received a pension for soldiers. She was truly a patriotic veteran.

✳ Coordination and Subordination: The Compound-Complex Sentence

At times you may want to show the relationship of three or more ideas within one sentence. If that relationship involves two or more main ideas and one or more supporting ideas, the combination can be stated in a compound-complex sentence (two or more independent clauses and one or more dependent clauses).

Before he learned how to operate a computer,

dependent clause

he had trouble with his typewritten assignments,

independent clause

but now he produces clean, attractive material.

independent clause

In our previous discussion of the complex sentence, we presented this group of six sentences:

I was very upset. The Fourth of July fireworks were especially loud. My dog ran away. The animal control officer made his morning rounds. He found my dog in another part of town. I was relieved.

We then converted the group of six sentences to four:

I was very upset. Because the Fourth of July fireworks were especially loud, my dog ran away. When the animal control officer made his morning rounds, he found my dog in another part of town. I was relieved.

If we wanted to show an even closer relationship of ideas we could combine the two complex sentences in this way (the italicized sentence is compound-complex):

I was very upset. *Because the Fourth of July fireworks were especially loud, my dog ran away; but when the animal control officer made his morning rounds, he found my dog in another part of town.* I was relieved.

Punctuation of Complicated Compound or Compound-Complex Sentences

If a compound or compound-complex sentence has one or more commas in the first clause, you may want to use a semicolon before the coordinating conjunction between the two clauses. Its purpose is to show the reader very clearly the division between the two independent clauses. The preceding example illustrates this use of the semicolon.

Exercise 4   Combining Sentences: Compound-Complex

Combine each group of sentences into one compound-complex sentence. Use the rules of sentence combining and punctuation discussed in this chapter.

1. Helen Keller suffered a serious childhood illness. She became

   blind and deaf. At first her parents did not know what to do.

2. Her parents would not give up despite discouraging advice.

   They advertised for a teacher. A tutor named Anne Sullivan

   agreed to help.

3. Young Helen began to discover the world through her sense of touch. She learned the alphabet. She started connecting words with objects.

4. Her physical condition was irreversible. Her progress was rapid. In three years she could read Braille.

5. She could not talk. She used sign language for speech. She used a special typewriter to write.

6. She reached the age of ten. She took speech lessons from a teacher of the deaf. In six years she could speak well enough to be understood.

7. She attended college. She still needed help. Anne Sullivan continued as her tutor and interpreter.

8. She graduated from college with honors. She became involved in programs to help the deaf and blind communicate. She wrote books and articles about problems of the disabled.

9. The effects of World War II presented special problems. Helen Keller helped disabled people in other countries. She helped soldiers blinded in the war.

10. Helen Keller died in 1968. She had an international reputation as a humanitarian. Her books had been translated into more than fifty languages.

✳ Other Ways to Combine Ideas

In this chapter you have learned how to combine simple sentences into compound, complex, and compound-complex sentences that show the coordination and subordination of ideas. There are other methods of combining ideas. Here are four you may want to use in your own writing:

1. Use an **appositive,** which is a noun or a noun phrase that immediately follows a noun or pronoun and renames it.

   > Susan is the leading scorer on the team. Susan is a quick and strong player.

   > Susan, *a quick and strong player,* is the leading scorer on the team.

2. Use a **prepositional phrase,** a preposition followed by a noun or pronoun object.

   > Dolly Parton wrote a song about a coat. The coat had many colors.

   > Dolly Parton wrote a song about a coat *of many colors.*

3. Drop the subject in the sentence that follows, and combine the sentences.

   > Some items are too damaged for recycling. They must be disposed of.

   > Some items are too damaged for recycling *and* must be disposed of.

4. Use a **participial phrase,** a group of words that includes a participle, which is a verbal that usually ends in *-ing* or *-ed.*

   > John rowed smoothly. He reached the shore.

   > *Rowing smoothly,* John reached the shore.

✳ Omissions: When Parts Are Missing

Do not omit words that are needed to make your sentences clear and logical. Of the many types of undesirable construction in which necessary words are omitted, the following are the most common.

1. **Subjects.** Do not omit a necessary subject in a sentence with two verbs.

ILLOGICAL	The cost of the car was $12,000 but would easily last me through college. (subject of *last*)
LOGICAL	The cost of the car was $12,000, but the car would easily last me through college.

2. **Verbs.** Do not omit verbs that are needed because of a change in the number of the subject or a change of tense.

ILLOGICAL   The bushes were trimmed and the grass mowed. (verb of *grass*)

LOGICAL   The bushes were trimmed and the grass was mowed.

ILLOGICAL   True honesty always has and always will be admired by most people. (tense)

LOGICAL   True honesty always has been and always will be admired by most people.

3. ***That* as a conjunction**. The conjunction *that* should not be omitted from a dependent clause if there is danger of misreading the sentence.

MISLEADING   We believed Eric, if not stopped, would hurt himself. (*that* after *believed*)

CLEAR   We believed that Eric, if not stopped, would hurt himself.

4. **Prepositions.** Do not omit prepositions in idiomatic phrases, in expressions of time, and in parallel phrases.

ILLOGICAL   Weekends the campus is deserted. (time)

LOGICAL   During weekends the campus is deserted.

ILLOGICAL   I have neither love nor patience with untrained dogs. (parallel phrases)

LOGICAL   I have neither love for nor patience with untrained dogs.

ILLOGICAL   Glenda's illness was something we heard only after her recovery. (*about* after *heard*)

LOGICAL   Glenda's illness was something we heard about only after her recovery.

Exercise 5 Correcting Omissions

Identify the kinds of omissions by writing one of the following words in the blanks to the left: subject, verb, conjunction, preposition. Insert the necessary words in the sentences.

_____   1. Charles had neither love nor patience with small pets.

_____   2. Because he was careless, a branch caught on the trigger of his gun, and went off.

_____   3. In the newspaper, the radio, and TV, the
                         story was the same.

_____   4. We saw the car, if not stopped, would hit the
                         tree.

_____   5. Because Jim had not worked that summer,
                         money was scarce in the fall and expenses
                         burdensome.

_____   6. Harry's ignorance was one of the things that we
                         learned on the trip.

_____   7. We believed the lie, if not revealed, would
                         harm people.

_____   8. The truck was creeping up the hill, and had
                         no thought at all of the traffic behind.

_____   9. I do not believe and never have that a per-
                         son's life is not his or her own responsibility.

_____   10. When Joe got his second wind, his breathing
                         slowed, and was able to go on running with-
                         out fatigue.

✳ Variety in Sentences: Types, Order, Length, Beginnings

Sentences can be written in a variety of ways to achieve freshness
and clarity. Much of this polishing takes place during revision. Here
are a few techniques for the main variations.

Types

You have learned that all four types of sentences are sound. Your task
as a writer is to decide which one to use for a particular thought.
That decision may not be made until you revise your composition.
Then you can choose on the basis of the relationship of ideas:

> **Simple:** a single idea
> **Compound:** two closely related ideas
> **Complex:** one idea more important than the other
> **Compound-complex:** a combination of the two parts

These types were all covered in Chapter 3. This chapter provides further practice, as you combine sentences.

Order

You will choose the order of parts and information according to what you want to emphasize. Typically the most emphatic location is at the end of any unit.

Length

Uncluttered and direct, short sentences commonly draw attention. Because that focus occurs only when they stand out from longer sentences, however, you would usually avoid a series of short sentences.

Beginnings

A long series of sentences with each beginning containing a subject followed by a verb may become monotonous. Consider beginning sentences in different ways:

> **With a prepositional phrase:** *In the distance* a dog barked.
> **With a transitional connective (conjunctive adverb) such as *then, however,* or *therefore*:** *Then* the game was over.
> **With a coordinating conjunction such as *and* or *but*:** *But* no one moved for three minutes.
> **With a dependent clause:** *Although he wanted a new Corvette,* he settled for a used Ford Taurus.
> **With an adverb:** *Carefully* he removed the thorn from the lion's paw.

Exercise 6 Providing Sentence Variety

Revise the following passage to achieve better sentence variety through changes in types of sentences, order of information, length of sentences, and beginnings of sentences. Also, combine sentences for improved expression. Compare your revisions with those of others in your class. There is no single correct way of making these changes.

Power Rangers to the Rescue
Leewan Yeomans

I do promotions on the weekends for TV's "Power Rangers." I'm Trini. She's supposed to be Chinese. I'm Chinese-American, the

kids think I'm the real Ranger when I remove my mask. I've
never felt very much like a Ranger except for one occasion. It was
a weekend promotion, held at a park. We were doing our routine.
I looked around and saw a little boy collapse. He had probably
been in distress for a while. Wearing the mask, I could hardly see
anything. Anyway, this little boy was lying there, thrashing
around and trying to throw up. No one was doing anything. The
Pink Ranger started running around trying to find the child's parents. I ran over when no one came to the aid of the boy, took off
my mask, and put my finger in his mouth to clear his throat.
There I found the problem. He had been chewing on, or maybe
blowing, a long balloon. He had swallowed it. I pulled it out of his
throat. It was almost a foot long. The whole spectacle must have
looked like a magic trick. The child still wasn't breathing well.
The paramedics were called. They quickly helped him back to
good health. His parents, who lived across the street, came to
carry him home. We Rangers put our masks back on. The audience cheered us as if we had planned the whole scene. We re-
sumed our routine. It was just another day of work for the Power
Rangers.

✳ Chapter Review

Exercise 7 Combining Sentences

*Combine each pair of sentences into a single sentence by using any
pattern.*

1. Cobras are among the most feared of all snakes. They are not

   the deadliest of all snakes.

2. Cobras do not coil before they strike. They cannot strike for a long distance.

3. Cobras do not have a hood. They flatten their neck by moving their ribs when they are nervous or frightened.

4. Cobras inject venom with their fangs. They spit venom at their victims.

5. Human beings will not die from the venom that has been spit. It can cause blindness if it is not washed from the eyes.

6. A person can die from a cobra bite. Death may come in only a few hours.

7. Snake charmers have long worked with cobras. They use a snake, a basket, and a flute.

8. The snakes cannot *hear* the music. They respond to the rhythmic movements of the charmers.

9. The snake charmers are hardly ever in danger of being bitten. They defang the cobras or sew their mouths shut.

10. Most cobras will flee from people. They attack if they are cornered or if they are guarding their eggs.

11. The tiny mongoose is the enemy of the cobra. It uses its sharp teeth to kill the cobra.

Exercise 8 Combining Sentences

Combine each pair or group of sentences into a single sentence by using any pattern.

1. Romeo and Juliet were young. They fell in love.

2. Their families were feuding. Romeo and Juliet decided to run away.

3. They tried to trick their families. Their plans failed. They both died.

4. The contestant spun the wheel one more time. Vanna White clapped her hands with glee.

5. Only one letter remained. Pat Sajak encouraged the contestant.

6. The wheel stopped. The contestant lost his turn.

7. The audience groaned. Vanna White almost cried. Pat Sajak comforted her.

8. Several tabloids have reported that Elvis has not left us. He has been sighted in several parts of the country and even on other planets.

9. The tabloids report that the King is just tired and wants privacy. They give credit to unnamed reliable sources.

10. The central character of *The Old Man and the Sea* is Santiago. Santiago is a fisherman with a string of bad luck.

11. He catches a fish. He loses most of it to sharks.

12. He struggles courageously. He achieves a moral victory.

13. Santiago is a true hero. He obeys his code.

Exercise 9 Combining Sentences

Use appropriate methods to combine sentences as needed. Add and delete words sparingly.

Muhammad Ali was arguably the greatest heavyweight boxing champion. He won the title on four occasions. He loved to perform for the press. He made up sayings and poems about himself and his opponents. He once said he would "float like a butterfly and sting like a bee." Ali announced that he would win each fight. He even named the round. He became a Black Muslim. He refused induction into the armed services. He was convicted of a crime for having done so. As a result he lost his championship. Later the decision was reversed by the U.S. Supreme Court. He won back the championship by defeating George Foreman in 1974. In 1978 he lost it to Leon Spinks. He regained it the next year. He retired in 1980. He soon returned to the ring once more to fight for the championship. He quit for good.

✳ 5

Correcting Fragments, Comma Splices, and Run-Ons

In Chapters 1 and 2, you learned about parts of speech and subjects and verbs. In Chapters 3 and 4, you identified and wrote different kinds of sentences. With the information you now have, you will be able to spot and correct three problems that sometimes creep into what is otherwise good writing. Those problems are sentence fragments, comma splices, and run-on sentences.

✳ Fragments

A correct sentence signals completeness. The structure and punctuation provide those signals. For example, if I say to you, "She left in a hurry," you do not necessarily expect me to say anything else, but if I say, "In a hurry," you do. If I say, "Tomorrow I will give you a quiz on the reading assignment," and I leave the room, you will merely take note of my words. But if I say, "Tomorrow when I give you a quiz on the reading assignment," and leave the room, you will probably be annoyed, and you may even chase after me and ask me to finish my sentence. Those examples illustrate the difference between completeness and incompleteness.

A **fragment** is a word or group of words without a subject ("Is going to town."), without a verb ("He going to town."), or without both ("Going to town."). A fragment can also be a group of words with a subject and verb that cannot stand alone ("When he goes to town."). Although the punctuation signals a sentence (a capital letter at the beginning and a period at the end), the structure of a fragment signals incompleteness. If you were to say or write a fragment to someone, that person would expect you to go on and finish the idea.

56

Other specific examples of common unacceptable fragments are the following:

- *Dependent clause only:* When she came.
- *Phrase(s) only:* Waiting there for some help.
- *No subject in main clause:* Went to the library.
- *No verb in main clause:* She being the only person there.

Dependent Clauses as Fragments: Clauses with Subordinating Conjunctions

In Chapter 3, you learned that words like *because, after, although, since,* and *before* (see page 28 for a more complete list) are subordinating conjunctions, words that show the relationship of a dependent clause to an independent one. A dependent clause punctuated like a sentence (capital letter at the beginning; period at the end) is a sentence fragment.

> *While the ship was sinking.*

You can choose one of many ways to fix that kind of fragment.

INCORRECT	They continued to dance. *While the ship was sinking.*
CORRECT	They continued to dance *while the ship was sinking.*
CORRECT	*While the ship was sinking,* they continued to dance.
CORRECT	The ship was sinking. They continued to dance.
CORRECT	The ship was sinking; they continued to dance.

In the first two correct sentences above, the dependent clause *while the ship was sinking* has been attached to an independent clause. In the next two sentences, the subordinating conjunction *while* has been omitted. The two independent clauses can then stand alone as sentences or as parts of a sentence, joined by a semicolon.

Dependent Clauses as Fragments: Clauses with Relative Pronouns

You also learned in Chapter 3 that words like *that, which,* and *who* can function as relative pronouns, words that relate a clause back to a noun or pronoun in the sentence. Relative clauses are dependent.

If they are punctuated as sentences (begin with a capital letter; end with a period), they are incorrect. They are really sentence fragments.

> *Which is lying on the floor.*

The best way to fix such a fragment is to attach it as closely as possible to the noun to which it refers.

INCORRECT	That new red sweater is mine. *Which is lying on the floor.*
CORRECT	The new red sweater, *which is lying on the floor,* is mine.

Reminder: Some relative clauses are restrictive (necessary to the meaning of the sentence) and should not be set off with commas. Some are nonrestrictive (not necessary to the meaning of the sentence), like the example above, and are set off by commas.

Phrases as Fragments

Although a phrase may carry an idea, a phrase is a fragment because it is incomplete in structure. It lacks both a subject and a verb. In Chapter 2 we looked at verbal phrases and prepositional phrases, and in Chapter 4 we briefly discussed appositive phrases.

Verbal Phrase

INCORRECT	*Having studied hard all evening.* John decided to retire.
CORRECT	*Having studied hard all evening,* John decided to retire.

The italicized part of the incorrect example is a verbal phrase. As you learned in Chapter 2, a verbal is verblike without being a verb in sentence structure. Verbals include verb parts of speech ending in *-ed* and *-ing.* To correct a verbal phrase fragment, attach it to a complete sentence (independent clause). When the phrase begins the sentence, it is usually set off by a comma.

Prepositional Phrase

INCORRECT	*After the last snow.* The workers built the road.
CORRECT	*After the last snow,* the workers built the road.

In this example, the fragment is a prepositional phrase—a group of words beginning with a preposition, such as *in, on, of, at,* and *with,* that connects a noun or pronoun object to the rest of the sentence. To correct a prepositional phrase fragment, attach it to a complete sentence (independent clause). If the prepositional phrase is long and begins the sentence, it is usually set off by a comma.

Appositive Phrase

INCORRECT	He lived in the small town of Whitman. *A busy industrial center near Boston.* [nonessential]
CORRECT	He lived in the small town of Whitman, *a busy industrial center near Boston.*
INCORRECT	Many readers admire the work of the nineteenth-century American poet. *Emily Dickinson.* [essential]
CORRECT	Many readers admire the work of the nineteenth-century American poet *Emily Dickinson.*

In these examples, the fragment is an appositive phrase—a group of words following a noun or pronoun and renaming it. To correct an appositive phrase fragment, connect it to a complete sentence (an independent clause). An appositive phrase fragment is set off by a comma or by commas only if it is not essential to the sentence.

Fragments as Word Groups Without Subjects or Without Verbs

INCORRECT	John studied many long hours. *And received the highest grade in the class.* (without subject)
CORRECT	John studied many long hours *and received the highest grade in the class.*
INCORRECT	*Few children living in that section of the country.* (without verb)
CORRECT	*Few children live in that section of the country.*

Each conventional sentence must have an independent clause, meaning a word or a group of words that contains a subject and a verb and that can stand alone. As you may recall from the discussion of subjects in Chapter 2, a command or direction sentence, such as "Think," has an understood subject of *you.*

Acceptable Fragments

Sometimes, fragments are used intentionally. When we speak, we often use the following fragments.

- *Interjections:* Great! Hooray! Whoa!
- *Exclamations:* What a day! How terrible! What a bother!
- *Greetings:* Hello. Good morning. Good night. Good evening.
- *Questions:* What for? Why not? Where to?
- *Informal conversation:* (What time is it?) Eight o'clock. Really.

In novels, plays, and short stories, fragments are often used in conversation among characters. However, unless you are writing fiction, you need to be able to identify fragments in your college assignments and turn those fragments into complete sentences.

Exercise 1 Identifying Fragments

Identify each of the following as a fragment (FRAG) or a complete sentence (OK).

_____   1. Asia, which developed much earlier than the West.

_____   2. More than five thousand years ago, Asia had an advanced civilization.

_____   3. People there who invented writing and created literature.

_____   4. Involved in the development of science, agriculture, and religion.

_____   5. The birthplace of the major religions of the world.

_____   6. The most common religion in Asia being Hinduism.

_____   7. The second most common religion is Islam.

_____   8. Asia is the most populous continent.

_____   9. With almost four billion people.

_____   10. Hong Kong and Bangladesh, which are among the most densely populated places in the world.

Exercise 2 Correcting Fragments

Underline and correct each fragment. Some items may be correct as is.

1. When Leroy Robert Paige was seven years old. He was carrying luggage at a railroad station in Mobile, Alabama.

2. He was a clever young fellow. Who invented a contraption for carrying four satchels (small suitcases) at one time.

3. After he did that. He was always known as Satchel Paige.

4. His fame rests on his being arguably the best baseball pitcher. Who ever played the game.

5. Because of the so-called Jim Crow laws. He, as an African American, was not allowed to play in the Major Leagues. Until 1948 after the Major League color barrier was broken.

6. By that time he was already forty-two. Although he was in excellent condition.

7. He had pitched. Wherever he could, mainly touring around the country.

8. When he faced Major Leaguers in exhibition games. He almost always won.

9. Because people liked to see him pitch. He pitched almost every day. While he was on tour.

10. One year he won 104 games. During his career he pitched 55 no-hitters and won more than 2,000 games.

11. He pitched his last game in the majors at the age of fifty-nine.

12. In 1971, he was the first African-American player. Who was voted into the Baseball Hall of Fame in a special category for those. Who played in the old Negro Leagues.

Exercise 3 Correcting Fragments

Underline and correct each fragment.

1. Although Woody Guthrie had a hard life. His songs are filled with hope.

2. His autobiography, *Bound for Glory,* tells of this free-spirited man. Who saw boomtown oil fields dry up and crops wither in the dust bowl.

3. Many people knew him only as the author of "This Land Is Your Land." Which is often treated as a second national anthem.

4. Because he was honest and would say what he thought. He was often out of work.

5. Cisco Houston said, "Woody is a man. Who writes two or three ballads before breakfast every morning."

6. The hobo, the migrant worker, the merchant marine, the sign painter, the labor agitator, the musician in New York City with

his hat on the sidewalk—Woody was a restless traveler. Whose life was as varied as his song bag.

7. Some of his best songs are about his experience during the days of the Great Depression. When he was an unofficial spokesperson for migrant workers in the West.

8. Arlo Guthrie, Woody's son, achieved his own fame. While he carried on the folk music tradition of his father.

9. Woody's song "Pretty Boy Floyd" was recorded by Bob Dylan. Who modeled his early style on that of Woody and once referred to himself as a "Woody Guthrie jukebox."

10. A simple farmer once said to a reporter, "I'll always remember Woody as the man. Who said, 'Some men will rob you with a six-gun and some with a fountain pen.'"

Exercise 4 Correcting Fragments

Correct the fragments in any way you wish. Many can be fixed by combining word groups in this list. Write your complete sentences in the spaces that follow.

1. Asia having many ethnic groups.

2. Including the Chinese, the Indians, the Arabs, the Turks, and the Jews.

3. The Chinese have different groups.

4. Speaking many dialects.

5. Although they have different dialects.

6. There is a national language.

7. A language called Mandarin.

8. Cultural differences exist in Taiwan.

9. The main difference being between the Chinese from the mainland and the Taiwanese.

10. Despite the differences, all Chinese have much culture in common.

✳ Comma Splices and Run-Ons

The comma splice and the run-on are two other kinds of faulty "sentences" that give false signals to the reader. In each instance the punctuation suggests that there is only one sentence, but, in fact, there is material for two.

The **comma splice** consists of two independent clauses with only a comma between them:

> *The weather was disappointing,* <u>we canceled the picnic.</u> (A comma by itself cannot join two independent clauses.)

The **run-on** differs from the comma splice in only one respect: it has no comma between the independent clauses. Therefore, the run-on is two independent clauses with *nothing* between them:

> *The weather was disappointing* <u>we canceled the picnic.</u> (Independent clauses must be properly connected.)

Because an independent clause can stand by itself as a sentence and because two independent clauses must be properly linked, you can use a simple technique to identify the comma splice and the run-on. If you see a sentence that you think may contain one of these two errors, ask yourself this question: "Can I insert a period at some place in the word group and still have a sentence on either side?" If the answer is yes and there is no word such as *and* or *but* following the inserted period, then you have a comma splice or a run-on to correct. In our previous examples of the comma splice and the run-on, we could insert a period after the word *disappointing* in each case, and we would still have an independent clause—therefore, a sentence—on either side.

Correcting Comma Splices and Run-Ons

Once you identify a comma splice or a run-on in your writing, you need to correct it. Use one of these four different ways to fix these common sentence problems: use a comma and a coordinating conjunction, use a subordinating conjunction, use a semicolon, or make each clause a separate sentence.

Use a Comma and a Coordinating Conjunction

INCORRECT   We canceled the picnic the weather was
             disappointing. (run-on)

CORRECT   We canceled the picnic, *for* the weather was
             disappointing. (Here we inserted a comma and the
             coordinating conjunction *for*.)

Knowing the seven coordinating conjunctions will help you in writing sentences and correcting sentence problems. Remember the acronym FANBOYS: *for, and, nor, but, or, yet, so.*

Exercise 5 Correcting Comma Splices and Run-Ons

Identify each word group as a comma splice (CS), a run-on (RO), or a complete sentence (OK), and correct the errors using commas and coordinating conjunctions.

EXAMPLE   ___CS___He did the assignment,^and his boss gave him a bonus.

_____   1. In 1846, a group of eighty-two settlers headed for California with much optimism, a hard road lay ahead.

_____   2. They had expected to cross the mountains before winter they were in good spirits.

_____   3. They would not arrive in California before winter, nor would some of them get there at all.

_____   4. When they encountered a heavy snowstorm, they stopped to spend the winter they still thought they would be safe.

_____ 5. They made crude shelters of logs and branches some also used moss and earth.

_____ 6. They had trouble managing, they had not encountered such problems before.

_____ 7. They ran out of regular food they ate roots, mice, shoe leather, and their horses.

_____ 8. Thirty-five members of the Donner Party died that winter the survivors were so hungry that they ate the dead bodies.

_____ 9. They were weak, sick, and depressed they did not give up.

_____ 10. Fifteen people set out to get help seven survived and returned to rescue friends and relatives.

Exercise 6 Correcting Comma Splices and Run-Ons

Identify each word group as a comma splice (CS), a run-on (RO), or a complete sentence (OK), and correct the errors using commas and coordinating conjunctions.

_____ 1. Comedian Woody Allen once observed that no one gets out of this world alive, we all know that no human is immortal.

_____ 2. But several famous dead people have managed to continue to *look* alive they (or their admirers) had their bodies preserved and put on display.

_____ 3. Philosopher Jeremy Bentham wanted his body preserved, his wishes were carried out when he died in 1832.

_____ 4. Bentham left a lot of money to London's University College, the college couldn't have the money unless it agreed to let Bentham's body attend its annual board of directors meetings.

_____ 5. Bentham's dressed-up body was posed sitting in an armchair in his hand was his favorite walking stick.

_____ 6. Every year for ninety-two years, the college complied with Bentham's instructions the board's minutes for those years record Bentham as "present but not voting."

_____ 7. Bentham's body is still at University College, it's on display now in a permanent exhibit.

_____ 8. V. I. Lenin, leader of the former Soviet Union, has been dead and on display since 1924 Russians and tourists can still visit his lifelike body enclosed in a glass coffin in Moscow.

_____ 9. The corpse of People's Republic of China founder Mao Zedong was preserved for posterity, too, in his mausoleum, an elevator raises his glass coffin from underground to a public viewing area every morning.

_____ 10. Other famous people turned into modern mummies were national leaders Joseph Stalin, Eva Perón, and Ho Chi Minh, and opera singer Enrico Caruso.

Use a Subordinating Conjunction

INCORRECT   The weather was disappointing, we canceled the picnic.

CORRECT   *Because* the weather was disappointing, we canceled the picnic.

By inserting the subordinating conjunction *because,* you can transform the first independent clause into a dependent clause and correct the comma splice. Knowing common subordinating conjunctions will help you in writing sentences and correcting sentence problems. Here is a list of the subordinating conjunctions you saw in Chapters 3 and 4. Each of these words indicates a particular relationship between the ideas being connected.

after	if	until
although	in order that	when
as	provided that	whenever
as if	rather than	where
because	since	whereas
before	so that	wherever
even if	than	whether
even though	unless	while

Exercise 7 Correcting Comma Splices and Run-Ons

Identify each word group as a comma splice (CS), a run-on (RO), or a complete sentence (OK), and correct the errors by making a dependent clause.

_____ 1. Jesse Owens won four gold medals in the 1936 Olympics he became a famous person.

_____ 2. The 1936 Olympics were held in Nazi Germany Owens was placed at a disadvantage.

_____ 3. Hitler believed in the superiority of the Aryans, he thought Owens would lose.

_____ 4. Jesse Owens won Hitler showed his disappointment openly.

_____ 5. Owens broke a record for the 200-meter race that had stood for thirty-six years.

_____ 6. Owens then jumped a foot farther than others in the long jump Hitler left the stadium.

_____ 7. Before the day was at last over, Owens had also won gold medals in the 100-meter dash and the 400-meter relay.

_____ 8. Hitler's early departure was a snub at Owens, but Jesse did not care.

_____ 9. Owens returned to the United States, he engaged in numerous exhibitions, including racing against a horse.

_____ 10. In his later years Owens became an official for the U.S. Olympic committee, he never received the recognition that many contemporary athletes do.

Exercise 8 Correcting Comma Splices and Run-Ons

Identify each word group as a comma splice (CS), a run-on (RO), or a complete sentence (OK), and correct the errors by making a dependent clause.

_____ 1. Chris Evert was one of the most successful tennis players of the 1970s and 1980s, she was not physically powerful.

_____ 2. She was intelligent and well coordinated, she became a top player.

_____ 3. She was still in her teens she won major championships.

_____ 4. She attracted much attention in 1974 she won fifty-five consecutive matches.

_____ 5. She reached the top, she had much competition there.

_____ 6. Evonne Goolagong was Evert's main competition at first Martina Navratilova soon assumed that role.

_____ 7. Financially Chris Evert's career was notable she made more than six million dollars.

_____ 8. Chris Evert helped to make women's tennis what it is today, she will not be forgotten.

_____ 9. She was called the "ice princess" she did not show her emotions.

_____ 10. She is regarded as one of the greatest athletes of the past forty years.

Use a Semicolon

INCORRECT	The weather was disappointing, we canceled the picnic.
CORRECT	The weather was disappointing; we canceled the picnic.
CORRECT	The weather was disappointing; *therefore,* we canceled the picnic.

This comma splice was corrected by a semicolon. The first correct example shows the semicolon alone. The second correct example shows a semicolon followed by the conjunctive adverb *therefore.* The conjunctive adverb is optional, but, as we have already seen, conjunctive adverbs can make the relationship between independent clauses stronger. Here is the list of conjunctive adverbs you saw in Chapter 4.

however	on the other hand
otherwise	then
therefore	consequently
similarly	also
hence	thus

Recall the acronym HOTSHOT CAT, made up of the first letter of each of these common conjunctive adverbs. The acronym will help you remember them. Other conjunctive adverbs include *in fact, for example, moreover, nevertheless, furthermore, now,* and *soon.*

Exercise 9   Correcting Comma Splices and Run-Ons

Identify each word group as a comma splice (CS), a run-on (RO), or a complete sentence (OK). Correct the errors with a semicolon, and add a conjunctive adverb if appropriate.

_____   1. Ants are highly social insects they live in colonies.

_____   2. They work for the benefit of the group each individual is important.

_____   3. Ants have different roles they will, in some species, have different sizes and shapes.

_____ 4. An ant will be a queen, a worker, or a male, there is not an identity problem among ants.

_____ 5. A worker may be a soldier whose job is to defend the nest that ant has large mandibles, or teeth.

_____ 6. The worker that is a janitor will have the job of cleaning the nest her head is big for pushing waste material through the tunnel.

_____ 7. The queen is very large because she must lay many eggs.

_____ 8. The workers are all female, their job is to do all of the work.

_____ 9. The males have only one function, and that function is to mate with the queen.

_____ 10. In some species, the workers may change roles in their work the males only mate and die young.

Make Each Clause a Separate Sentence

INCORRECT   The weather was disappointing, we canceled the picnic.

CORRECT   The weather was disappointing. We canceled the picnic.

To correct the comma splice, replace the comma with a period, and begin the second sentence (the second independent clause) with a capital letter. This method is at once the simplest and most common method of correcting comma splices and run-ons. For a run-on, insert a period between the two independent clauses and begin the second sentence with a capital letter.

Exercise 10 Correcting Comma Splices and Run-Ons

Identify each word group as a comma splice (CS), a run-on (RO), or a complete sentence (OK). Correct the errors with a period and a capital letter.

_____ 1. The world's fastest steel track roller coaster is the Top Thrill Dragster it's at the Cedar Point Amusement Park in Ohio.

_____ 2. Riders rocket out of a starting gate they reach a speed of 120 miles per hour in four seconds.

_____ 3. The second-fastest roller coaster is in Japan it goes a mere 106.8 miles per hour.

_____ 4. Wooden roller coasters are downright pokey in comparison the fastest reaches speeds of only 78.3 miles per hour.

_____ 5. If you're looking for the biggest drop, the Top Thrill Dragster has that distinction, too.

_____ 6. The largest drop on the Top Thrill Dragster is 400 feet, compare that to the largest drop on a wooden coaster, which is only 214 feet.

_____ 7. The longest roller coaster ride of them all is the Steel Dragon 2000 in Japan that coaster is 8,133 feet long.

_____ 8. You want the steepest angle of descent you can choose from several steel track coasters that allow you to plummet downward at a 90-degree angle.

_____ 9. The steepest wooden coasters average about 55 degrees as a matter of fact, the steepest of all is only 61 degrees.

_____ 10. Most of the world's record-setting roller coasters were opened between 2000 and 2003 thrill-seekers hope they'll continue to get faster and steeper.

✳ **Chapter Review**

Exercise 11 Correcting Fragments, Comma Splices, and Run-Ons

Correct each fragment, comma splice, and run-on. Choose whichever method of correction works best for each sentence problem.

Deserts are often referred to as wastelands. It is true that not as many plants grow there as in temperate zones, it is also true that animals do not live there in great numbers. But many plants and animals live and do quite well in the desert. Because of their adaptations.

Not all deserts have the same appearance. Many people think of the desert as a hot, sandy area. Actually sand covers only about twenty percent of the desert. Some deserts have mountains some others have snow.

Because deserts are dry for most of the year. Plants must conserve and store water. Several kinds of cacti can shrink during a dry season and swell during a rainy season. Some shrubs simply drop their leaves and use their green bark to manufacture chlorophyll. Seeds sometimes lying in the desert for several years before sprouting to take advantage of a rainfall.

Animals have quite effectively adjusted to the desert, some animals obtain moisture from the food they eat and require no water. One animal of the desert, the camel, produces fat. Which it stores in its hump. The fat allows the camel to reserve more body heat it needs little water. Still other animals feed only at night or are inactive for weeks or even months.

About fifteen percent of the land of the earth is covered by deserts. That area increasing every year. Because of overgrazing by livestock. Also because of the destruction of forests. Areas that were once green and fertile will now support little life and only a small population of human beings.

6

Balancing Sentence Parts

We are surrounded by balance. Watch a colorful cross-frame, or diamond, kite as it soars in the sky. If you draw an imaginary line from the top to the bottom of the kite, you will see corresponding parts on either side. If you were to replace one of the sides with a loose-flapping fabric, the kite would never fly. A similar lack of balance can also cause a sentence to crash.

Consider these statements:

"*To be* or not *to be*—that is the question." (dash added)

This line from *Hamlet,* by William Shakespeare, is one of the most famous in literature. Compare it to the well-balanced kite in a strong wind. Its parts are parallel and it "flies" well.

"*To be* or *not being*—that is the question."

It still vaguely resembles the sleek kite, but now the second phrase causes it to dip like an unbalanced kite. Lurching, the line begins to lose altitude.

"*To be* or *death is the other alternative*—that is the question."

The line slams to the floor. Words scatter across the carpet. We go back to the revision board.

The first sentence is forceful and easy to read. The second is more difficult to follow. The third is almost impossible to understand. We understand it only because we know what it should look like from having read the original. The point is that perceptive readers are as critical of sentences as kite-watchers are of kites.

※ Basic Principles of Parallelism

Parallelism as it relates to sentence structure is usually achieved by joining words with similar words: nouns with nouns, adjectives (words that can describe nouns) with adjectives, adverbs (words that can describe verbs) with adverbs, and so forth.

> *Men, women,* and *children* enjoy the show. (nouns)
>
> The players are *excited, eager,* and *enthusiastic.* (adjectives)
>
> The author wrote *skillfully* and *quickly.* (adverbs)

Parallel structure may also be achieved by joining groups of words with other similar groups of words: prepositional phrase with prepositional phrase, clause with clause, sentence with sentence.

> She fell *in love* and *out of love* in a few minutes. (prepositional phrases)
>
> *Who he was* and *where he came from* did not matter. (clauses)
>
> *He came in a hurry. He left in a hurry.* (sentences)

Parallelism means balancing one structure with another of the same kind. Faulty parallel structure is awkward and draws unfavorable attention to what is being said.

> NONPARALLEL   Tim Duncan's reputation is based on his ability in *passing, shooting,* and *he is good at rebounds.*
>
> PARALLEL   Tim Duncan's reputation is based on his ability in *passing, shooting,* and *rebounding.*

The words *passing* and *shooting* are of the same kind (verblike words used as nouns), but the rest of the sentence is different. You don't have to know terms to realize that there is a problem in smoothness and emphasis. Just read the material aloud. Then compare it with the parallel statement; *he is good at rebounds* is changed to *rebounding* to make a sentence that's easy on the eye and ear.

✳ Signal Words

Some words signal parallel structure. If you use *and,* the items joined by *and* should almost always be parallel. If they aren't, then *and* is probably inappropriate.

> The weather is hot *and* humid. (*and* joins adjectives)
>
> The car *and* the trailer are parked in front of the house. (*and* joins nouns)

The same principle is true for *but,* although it implies a direct contrast. Where contrasts are being drawn, parallel structure is essential to clarify those contrasts.

> He *purchased* a Dodger Dog, *but* I *chose* the Stadium Peanuts. (*but* joins contrasting clauses)
>
> She *made* an A in math *but failed* her art class. (*but* joins contrasting verbs)

You should regard all the coordinating conjunctions (FANBOYS) as signals for parallel structure.

Exercise 1 Identifying Signal Words and Parallel Elements

Underline the parallel elements—words, phrases, or clauses— and circle the signal words in the following sentences. The sentences in these exercises are based on video-review excerpts from Movie Guide *by the Wherehouse; the film titles are shown in parentheses.*

EXAMPLE   One by one they are <u>stalked</u>, <u>terrorized</u>, (and) <u>murdered</u>. (*The Howling*)

1. The residents become the target of vicious, relentless, and inexplicable attacks by hordes of birds. (*The Birds*)

2. A family moves into a supposedly haunted New York home, and they find that the house is inoperative. (*The Amityville Horror*)

3. While they try to make a comfortable life for themselves and to ignore a few irritations, all hell breaks loose.

4. Muffy invited her college friends to her parents' secluded island home but neglected to tell them it might be the last day of their lives. (*April Fool's Day*)

5. A woman discovers that her young daughter has an inherent evil streak and has caused the death of several people. (*The Bad Seed*)

6. A physician surgically separates Siamese twins and is hated by them. (*Basket Case*)

7. One twin is normal, and the other is horribly deformed.

8. The deformed twin becomes an embittered and vindictive person.

9. In a final unreasoning, angry, and brutal assault, she rips the face off the doctor.

10. A slimy alien crashes to earth and devours everyone in its path. (*The Blob*)

✳ Combination Signal Words

The words *and* and *but* are the most common individual signal words used with parallel constructions. Sometimes, however, **combination words** signal the need for parallelism or balance. The most common ones are *either/or, neither/nor, not only/but also, both/and,* and *whether/or.* Now consider the following faulty sentences and two types of corrections:

NONPARALLEL   *Either* we will win this game, *or* let's go out
              fighting.

PARALLEL   *Either we will* win this game, *or we will* go out
              fighting.

The correction is made by changing *let's* to *we will* to parallel the *we will* in the first part of the sentence. The same construction should follow the *either* and the *or.*

NONPARALLEL	Flour is used *not only* to bake cakes *but also* in paste.
PARALLEL	Flour is used *not only to bake* cakes *but also to make* paste.

The correction is made by changing *in* (a preposition) to *to make* (an infinitive). Now an infinitive follows both *not only* and *but also.*

Exercise 2   Identifying Combination Signal Words and Parallel Elements

Underline the parallel elements—words, phrases, or clauses—and circle the combination signal words in the following sentences.

1. Robin Hood not only robbed from the rich but also gave to the poor. (*Adventures of Robin Hood,* 1938)

2. Both Humphrey Bogart and Katharine Hepburn star in this movie about two unlikely people traveling together through the jungle rivers of Africa during World War I. (*The African Queen*)

3. Dr. Jekyll discovers a potion, and now he can be either himself or Mr. Hyde. (*Dr. Jekyll and Mr. Hyde*)

4. An Oklahoma family moves to California and finds neither good jobs nor compassion in the "promised land." (*The Grapes of Wrath*)

5. In this Christmas classic, Jimmy Stewart stars as a man who can either die by suicide or go back to see what life would have been like without him. (*It's a Wonderful Life*)

6. During the Korean War, army surgeons discover that they must either develop a lunatic lifestyle or go crazy. (*M*A*S*H*)

7. An advertising executive not only gets tied up with an obnoxious and boring salesman but also goes with him on a wacky chase across the country. (*Planes, Trains, and Automobiles*)

8. In this flawless integration of animation and live action, Roger and Eddie try to discover both who framed Roger and who is playing patty-cake with his wife. (*Who Framed Roger Rabbit?*)

9. A long-suffering black woman named Celie experiences not only heartaches but also some joy as she rises from tragedy to personal triumph. (*The Color Purple*)

10. An independent man learns that he is expected to give up either his dignity or his life. (*Cool Hand Luke*)

✳ Chapter Review

Exercise 3 Completing Sentences with Parallel Elements

Complete each of the following sentences by adding a word, phrase, or clause that is parallel to the italicized word, phrase, or clause.

1. We went to the zoo not only for *fun* but also for _____

_____

2. He attended Utah State University for *a good education* and __

_____

3. For a college major, she was considering *English, history,* and

   _____

4. Mr. Ramos was a *good neighbor* and _____

   _____

5. My diet for breakfast that week consisted of *a slice of bread, a glass of low-fat milk,* and _____

   _____

6. She decided that she must choose between *a social life* and ___

   _____

7. Either *she would make the choice,* or _____

   _____

8. Because we are mutually supportive, either *we will all have a good time,* or _____

   _____

9. Like the Three Musketeers, our motto is *"All for one,* and_____

   _____

10. My intention was to *work a year, save my money,* and_____

   _____

Exercise 4 Writing Sentences with Parallel Elements

Use each of the following signal words or combined signal words in a sentence about the topic food.

1. and _____

   _____

2. but _____

   _____

3. so _____

   _____

4. either/or _____

_____

5. both/and _____

_____

7

Verbs

This chapter covers the use of standard verbs. To some, the word *standard* implies "correct." A more precise meaning is "that which is conventional among educated people." Therefore, a standard verb is the right choice in most school assignments, most published writing, and most important public speaking situations. We all change our language when we move from these formal occasions to informal ones: we don't talk to our families in the same way we would speak at a large gathering in public; we don't write letters to friends the same way we write a history report. But even with informal language we would seldom change from standard to nonstandard usage.

✳ Regular and Irregular Verbs

Verbs can be divided into two categories, called *regular* and *irregular*. Regular verbs are predictable, but irregular verbs—as the term suggests—follow no definite pattern.

Verbs always show time. Present-tense verbs show an action or a state of being that is occurring at the present time: I *like* your hat. He *is* at a hockey game right now. Present-tense verbs can also imply a continuation from the past into the future: She *drives* to work every day.

Past-tense verbs show an action or a state of being that occurred in the past: We *walked* to town yesterday. Tim *was* president of the club last year.

Regular Verbs
Present Tense

For *he, she,* and *it,* regular verbs in the present tense add an *-s* or an *-es* to the base word. The following chart shows the present tense of the base word *ask,* which is a regular verb.

	Singular	**Plural**
FIRST PERSON	I ask	we ask
SECOND PERSON	you ask	you ask
THIRD PERSON	he, she, it asks	they ask

If the verb ends in *-y,* you might have to drop the *-y* and add *-ies* for *he, she,* and *it.*

	Singular	**Plural**
FIRST PERSON	I try	we try
SECOND PERSON	you try	you try
THIRD PERSON	he, she, it tries	they try

Past Tense

For regular verbs in the past tense, add *-ed* to the base form:

Base Form (Present)	**Past**
walk	walked
answer	answered

If the base form already ends in *-e,* add just *-d:*

Base Form (Present)	**Past**
smile	smiled
decide	decided

If the base form ends in a consonant followed by *-y,* drop the *-y* and add *-ied.*

Base Form (Present)	**Past**
fry	fried
amplify	amplified

Regardless of how you form the past tense, regular verbs in the past tense do not change forms. The following chart shows the past tense of the base word *like,* which is a regular verb.

	Singular	**Plural**
FIRST PERSON	I liked	we liked
SECOND PERSON	you liked	you liked
THIRD PERSON	he, she, it liked	they liked

Past Participles

The past participle uses the helping verbs *has*, *have*, or *had* along with the past tense of the verb. For regular verbs, the past-participle form of the verb is the same as the past tense.

Base Form	Past	Past Participle
happen	happened	happened
hope	hoped	hoped
cry	cried	cried

Following is a list of some common regular verbs, showing the base form, the past tense, and the past participle. The base form can also be used with such helping verbs as *can, could, do, does, did, may, might, must, shall, should, will,* and *would.*

Regular Verbs

Base Form (Present)	Past	Past Participle
ask	asked	asked
answer	answered	answered
cry	cried	cried
decide	decided	decided
dive	dived (dove)	dived
drag	dragged	dragged
finish	finished	finished
happen	happened	happened
learn	learned	learned
like	liked	liked
love	loved	loved
need	needed	needed
open	opened	opened
start	started	started
suppose	supposed	supposed
walk	walked	walked
want	wanted	wanted

Irregular Verbs

Irregular verbs do not follow any definite pattern.

Base Form (Present)	Past	Past Participle
shake	shook	shaken
make	made	made
begin	began	begun

Some irregular verbs that sound similar in the present tense don't follow the same pattern.

Base Form (Present)	Past	Past Participle
ring	rang	rung
swing	swung	swung
bring	brought	brought

Present Tense

For *he, she,* and *it,* irregular verbs in the present tense add an *-s* or an *-es* to the base word. The following chart shows the present tense of the base word *break,* which is an irregular verb.

	Singular	Plural
FIRST PERSON	I break	we break
SECOND PERSON	you break	you break
THIRD PERSON	he, she, it breaks	they break

If the irregular verb ends in *-y,* you might have to drop the *-y* and add *-ies* for *he, she,* and *it.*

	Singular	Plural
FIRST PERSON	I fly	we fly
SECOND PERSON	you fly	you fly
THIRD PERSON	he, she, it flies	they fly

Past Tense

Like past-tense regular verbs, past-tense irregular verbs do not change their forms. The following chart shows the past tense of the irregular verb *do.*

	Singular	Plural
FIRST PERSON	I did	we did
SECOND PERSON	you did	you did
THIRD PERSON	he, she, it did	they did

Past Participles

Following is a list of some common irregular verbs, showing the base form (present), the past tense, and the past participle.

Like regular verbs, the base forms can be used with such helping verbs as *can, could, do, does, did, may, might, must, shall, should, will,* and *would.*

Irregular Verbs

Base Form (Present)	Past	Past Participle
arise	arose	arisen
awake	awoke (awaked)	awaked
be	was, were	been
become	became	become
begin	began	begun
bend	bent	bent
blow	blew	blown
break	broke	broken
bring	brought	brought
buy	bought	bought
catch	caught	caught
choose	chose	chosen
cling	clung	clung
come	came	come
creep	crept	crept
deal	dealt	dealt
do	did	done
drink	drank	drunk
drive	drove	driven
eat	ate	eaten
feel	felt	felt
fight	fought	fought
fling	flung	flung
fly	flew	flown
forget	forgot	forgotten
freeze	froze	frozen
get	got	got (gotten)
go	went	gone
grow	grew	grown
have	had	had
know	knew	known
lead	led	led
leave	left	left
lose	lost	lost
mean	meant	meant

(continued)

Base Form (Present)	Past	Past Participle
read	read	read
ride	rode	ridden
ring	rang	rung
see	saw	seen
shine	shone	shone
shine	shined	shined
shoot	shot	shot
sing	sang	sung
sink	sank	sunk
sleep	slept	slept
slink	slunk	slunk
speak	spoke	spoken
spend	spent	spent
steal	stole	stolen
stink	stank (stunk)	stunk
sweep	swept	swept
swim	swam	swum
swing	swung	swung
take	took	taken
teach	taught	taught
tear	tore	torn
think	thought	thought
throw	threw	thrown
wake	woke (waked)	woken (waked)
weep	wept	wept
write	wrote	written

✳ "Problem" Verbs

The following pairs of verbs are especially troublesome and confusing: *lie* and *lay, sit* and *set,* and *rise* and *raise.* One way to tell them apart is to remember which word in each pair takes a direct object. A direct object answers the question *whom* or *what* in connection with a verb. The words *lay, raise,* and *set* take a direct object.

He *raised* the window. (He *raised* what?)

Lie, rise, and *sit,* however, cannot take a direct object. We cannot say, for example, "He rose the window." In the following examples, the italicized words are objects.

Present Tense	Meaning	Past Tense	Past Participle	Example
lie	to rest	lay	lain	I lay down to rest.
lay	to place something	laid	laid	We laid the *books* on the table.
rise	to go up	rose	risen	The smoke rose quickly.
raise	to lift	raised	raised	She raised the *question*.
sit	to rest	sat	sat	He sat in the chair.
set	to place something	set	set	They set the *basket* on the floor.

✳ The Twelve Verb Tenses at a Glance

Some languages, such as Chinese and Navajo, have no verb tenses to indicate time. English has a fairly complicated system of tenses, but most verbs pattern in what are known as the simple tenses: past, present, and future. Altogether there are twelve tenses in English. The following charts present those tenses in sentences, explain what the different tenses mean, and show how to form them.

Simple Tenses

PRESENT (may imply a continuation from past to future) — I, we, you, they *drive.* He, she, it *drives.*

PAST — I, we, you, he, she, it, they *drove.*

FUTURE — I, we, you, he, she, it, they *will drive.*

Perfect Tenses

PRESENT PERFECT (completed recently in the past; may continue into the present) — I, we, you, they *have driven.* He, she, it *has driven.*

PAST PERFECT (completed prior to a specific time in the past) — I, we, you, he, she, it, they *had driven.*

FUTURE PERFECT (will occur at a time prior to a specific time in the future)	I, we, you, he, she, it, they *will have driven.*

Progressive Tenses

PRESENT PROGRESSIVE (in progress now)	I *am driving.* He, she, it *is driving.* You, they *are driving.*
PAST PROGRESSIVE (in progress in the past)	I, he, she, it *was driving.* You, they *were driving.*
FUTURE PROGRESSIVE (in progress in the future)	I, you, he, she, it, they *will be driving.*

Perfect Progressive Tenses

PRESENT PERFECT PROGRESSIVE (in progress up to now)	I, you, they *have been driving.* He, she, it *has been driving.*
PAST PERFECT PROGRESSIVE (in progress before another event in the past)	I, you, he, she, it, they *had been driving.*
FUTURE PERFECT PROGRESSIVE (in progress before another event in the future)	I, you, he, she, it, they *will have been driving.*

❋ Community Dialects and Standard Usage

Community dialects may be highly expressive and colorful. Popular songs and many television programs often use them well. Some people who use only a community dialect are much more gifted in communicating—explaining things, telling a story, getting to the point—than those who use only the standard dialect. And some people can use either the standard or the community dialect with equal skill. Those people are, in a limited sense, bilingual.

That said, we turn to our concern in this book, the standard use of language—and, specifically in this chapter, the standard use of verbs. Standard usage is advantageous because it is appropriate for the kind of writing and speaking you are likely to do in pursuing your college work and future career.

The following patterns will show the difference between a community dialect and the standard dialect for a regular verb *(walk)* and three irregular verbs *(do, be,* and *have).*

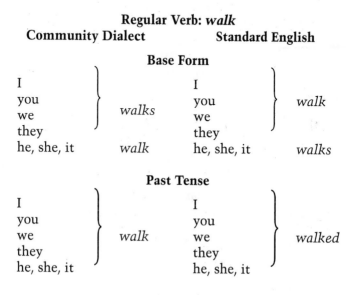

Regular Verb: *walk*

Community Dialect		Standard English	
Base Form			
I you we they	walks	I you we they	walk
he, she, it	walk	he, she, it	walks
Past Tense			
I you we they he, she, it	walk	I you we they he, she, it	walked

Regular Verb: *do*

Community Dialect		Standard English	
Base Form			
I you we they	does	I you we they	do
he, she, it	do	he, she, it	does
Past Tense			
I you we they he, she, it	done	I you we they he, she, it	did

Irregular Verb: *be*

Community Dialect   **Standard English**

Base Form

Community Dialect		Standard English	
I		I	*am*
you		you	
we	*be, is,* or	we	*are*
they	no verb	they	
he, she, it		he, she, it	*is*

Past Tense

Community Dialect		Standard English	
I		I	
he, she, it	*were*	he, she, it	*was*
we		we	
you	*was*	you	*were*
they		they	

Irregular Verb: *have*

Community Dialect   **Standard English**

Base Form

Community Dialect		Standard English	
I		I	
you	*has*	you	*have*
we		we	
they		they	
he, she, it	*have*	he, she, it	*has*

Past Tense

Community Dialect		Standard English	
I		I	
you	*have*	you	
we	or	we	*had*
they	*has*	they	
he, she, it		he, she, it	

Exercise 1 Community Dialects: Selecting Verbs

Underline the standard English verb form.

1. I (talk, talks) fast at times. He (talk, talks) fast all the time.

2. I (talked, talks) to her on the phone. She (talked, talk) back.

3. We (talks, talked) about our secrets. We (talks, talked) softly.

4. We (walks, walked) home in the dark. I (walks, walked) in front.

5. I (walks, walk) fast when I am scared. She (walk, walks) fast all the time.

6. She (be, is) my best friend. I (be, am) her best friend.

7. We (be, is, are) very close. We (was, were) strangers last year.

8. At school, I (does, do) my work, and she (do, does) hers.

9. In the neighborhood, we (have, has) a close relationship. I (has, have) no need of other friends.

10. She (does, do) her school work each day. I (does, do) mine almost every day.

Exercise 2 Community Dialects: Selecting Verbs

Underline the standard English verb form.

1. My school mascot (be, is) a Mountaineer. He (is, be) a funny little figure of a man with a coonskin cap.

2. We (calls, call) him Mountie. I (like, likes) him very much.

3. He (be, is) no sex symbol. He (be, is) just a symbol of someone struggling to reach the top of a mountain.

4. He (don't, doesn't) have any pretensions. He always (have, has) a smile.

5. The Mountie logo (appears, appear) on many items. My favorite logo items (are, be, is) caps and t-shirts.

6. The Mountie (walks, walk) to the top of the mountain in education. The Mountie (play, plays) sports at the top of the league.

7. An hour ago, at the Mountie Grill, I (order, ordered) two Mountie Burgers and (paid, pay) good money for them.

8. They (be, are) a bargain at any price. I (washed, wash) them down with a thick Mountie Shake.

9. I soon (has, had) a Mountie stomach. It (be, was) full of Mountie gas.

10. I (walk, walked) to the Mountie Health Office. Where (be, is) a Mountie aspirin when you (need, needs) one?

Exercise 3 Selecting Verbs

Underline the standard English verb form.

1. This story is about Bill "Chick" Walker, who (lossed, lost) all he owned at the Wagon Wheel Saloon in Las Vegas.

2. Chick had (laid, layed) one thousand dollars on the red 21 at the roulette table.

3. For that spin, he (done, did) an amazing thing—he (won, wins).

4. But after a while, Chick (became, become) stupid, and his luck (ran, run) out.

5. Before he had (ate, eaten) breakfast, he accepted free drinks from the charming Trixie, who (served, serve) cocktails.

6. His judgment was soon (ruined, ruint) by the drinks, and he (put, putted) all his money on one spin.

7. That wager (cost, costed) Chick everything, and he couldn't (raise, rise) any more money.

8. Moreover, Trixie would not (sit, set) with him because she (like, liked) only winners.

9. Chick drained his glass, (rose, raised) from his red tufted vinyl barstool, and (head, headed) for the parking lot.

10. There he (known, knew) Bonnie Lou would be waiting for him because she (lust, lusted) for losers.

Exercise 4 Selecting Verbs

Underline the standard English verb form.

1. In the twentieth century, two jilted men on opposite sides of the country (create, created) amazing structures to soothe their broken hearts.

2. In 1908, Baldasare Forestiere (built, builded) a four-room underground apartment in Fresno, California.

3. Then he (goes, went) to his native Italy and (ask, asked) his childhood sweetheart to join him in America.

4. When she refused, a sorrowful Baldasare (returns, returned) to the United States and (threw, throwed) himself into his digging.

5. By the time Baldasare died in 1946, he had (digged, dug) for thirty-eight years and had (construct, constructed) ninety underground rooms over ten acres.

6. Just after World War II, Edward Leedskalnin (began, begins) building a castle from enormous coral rocks in Florida City, Florida.

7. He had been (jilted, jilten) in 1920 by his sixteen-year-old fiancée, Agnes.

8. Edward (hopes, hoped) that Agnes would come back to him when he (became, become) famous for his project, which he moved to Homestead, Florida.

9. Edward (works, worked) on his castle for sixteen years in the dark of night, and no one (knows, knowed) how the five-foot-tall man moved twenty-five-ton blocks.

10. Unfortunately, Agnes never (seen, saw) Coral Castle, and she did not (change, changed) her mind about marrying Edward.

Exercise 5 Selecting Verbs

Underline the standard English verb form.

1. Recycling is very important; almost nothing should be (throwed, thrown) away.

2. For instance, ties that are worn out can (become, became) tails for kites or leashes for dogs.

3. You may not have (realize, realized) that you can (use, used) toothbrushes to clean shoes.

4. I personally (raised, rose) vacation money by recycling lard for candles.

5. Your golfing pals will wonder why they've never (thinked, thought) of using their old socks as golf covers.

6. A clear, plastic yogurt lid can (become, became) a frame for a school photo if you add a magnet.

7. Bridesmaid dresses can be cut up and (sewed, sewn) together to create decorative throw pillows.

8. This textbook can be (used, use) to wrap fish.

9. Strapped to the chest, it can (stop, stopped) small-caliber bullets.

10. When (dropped, dropt) from sufficient height, a single copy has been (known, knowed) to kill small rodents.

Exercise 6 Selecting Verbs

Underline the standard English verb form.

1. According to legend, a vampire (lays, lies) in his coffin during the daylight hours.

2. Like a teenager, he (sets, sits) his own schedule: He sleeps all day and stays out all night.

3. He cannot (rise, raise) until after the sun sets.

4. Then the bloodsucker can (rise, raise) the coffin's lid and (set, sit) up.

5. He (rises, raises) from his bed hungry.

6. But don't bother (setting, sitting) a place for him at the dinner table.

7. He goes out hunting for victims who have unwisely (lain, laid) down their crucifixes, wooden stakes, and garlic necklaces.

8. He pounces quickly so that the victim has no time to (rise, raise) an alarm.

9. If he (lies, lays) his hands upon you, you're a goner.

10. But when the sun begins to (rise, raise) in the sky, this monster must hurry back to bed to (lie, lay) his head down.

Exercise 7 Choosing Verb Tense

Underline the correct verb tense.

1. We (study, are studying) William Shakespeare's play *Romeo and Juliet*.

2. The teenagers Romeo and Juliet (met, had met) at a party.

3. By the time the party was over, they (fell, had fallen) in love.

4. Unfortunately, though, their families (feud, were feuding), so Romeo and Juliet (hid, had hidden) their affection for one another.

5. They secretly (married, had married) and (planned, had planned) to run away together.

6. But long before Juliet met Romeo, Juliet's father (decided, had decided) that she would marry a man named Paris.

7. The night before her wedding, Juliet (took, had taken) a potion that made her appear dead.

8. This tale (has, has had) a tragic ending because before Romeo found Juliet in her tomb, he (was not informed, had not been informed) that she wasn't really dead.

9. So he (committed, had committed) suicide, and Juliet (stabbed, had stabbed) herself when she awoke to find his body.

10. If I read this story again, I (have, will have) a tissue ready to dry my tears.

Exercise 8 Choosing Verb Tense

Underline the correct verb tense.

1. By the time the game was over, most fans (left, had left).

2. The shipping clerks said they (had sent, sent) the package.

3. We (studied, are studying) the user's guide now.

4. We (decide, will decide) on the winner tomorrow.

5. They reminded us that we (made, had made) the same promise before.

6. Jill (had believed, believed) in his guilt until she saw the complete evidence.

7. Jake (had been napping, napped) when the alarm sounded.

8. By the time he finished talking, he realized that he (said, had said) too much.

9. At the end of the semester, the course grade (depends, will depend) on your ability to write well.

10. After he retired, I realized how much I (had learned, learned) from working with him.

Exercise 9 Using Verbs in Sentences

Use each of these words in a sentence of ten words or more.

1. *lie, lay* (rest), *lain, laid* _____

   _____

_____

_____

_____

_____

_____

2. *sit, sat, set* _____

_____

_____

_____

_____

_____

3. *is, was, were* _____

_____

_____

_____

_____

_____

4. *do, does* (or *don't, doesn't*) _____

_____

_____

_____

_____

_____

❋ Subject-Verb Agreement

The basic principle of **subject-verb agreement** is that if the subject
is singular, the verb should be singular, and if the subject is plural,
the verb should be plural. There are ten major guidelines to en-
sure number agreement between subjects and verbs. In the examples under the following guidelines, the correct subjects and verbs
are italicized.

1. Do not let words that come between the subject and verb affect
   agreement.

   - Modifying phrases and clauses frequently come between the
     subject and verb:

     The various *types* of drama *were* not *discussed.*

     Angela, who is hitting third, *is* the best player.

     The *price* of those shoes *is* too high.

   - Certain prepositions can cause trouble. The following words
     are prepositions, not conjunctions: *along with, as well as, be-
     sides, in addition to, including,* and *together with.* The words
     that function as objects of prepositions cannot also be sub-
     jects of the sentence.

     The *coach,* along with the players, *protests* the decision.

   - In compound subjects in which one subject is positive and
     one subject is negative, the verb agrees with the positive
     subject.

     Phillip, not the other boys, *was* the culprit.

2. Do not let inversions (verb before subject, not the normal order)
   affect the agreement of subject and verb.

   - Verbs and other words may come before the subject. Do not
     let them affect the agreement. To understand subject-verb re-
     lationships, recast the sentence in normal word order.

     Are Juan and his *sister* at home? (question form)

     Juan and his *sister are* at home. (normal order)

   - A sentence filler is a word that is grammatically independent
     of other words in the sentence. The most common fillers are
     there and *here.* Even though a sentence filler precedes the
     verb, it should not be treated as the subject.

There *are* many *reasons* for his poor work. (The verb *are* agrees with the subject *reasons.*)

3. A singular verb agrees with a singular indefinite pronoun. (See page 127.)

- Most indefinite pronouns are singular.

  Each of the women *is* ready at this time.

  Neither of the women *is* ready at this time.

  One of the children *is* not paying attention.

- Certain indefinite pronouns do not clearly express either a singular or plural number. Agreement, therefore, depends on the meaning of the sentence. These pronouns are *all, any, none,* and *some.*

  All of the melon *was* good.

  All of the melons *were* good.

  None of the pie *is* acceptable.

  None of the pies *are* acceptable.

4. Two or more subjects joined by *and* usually take a plural verb.

  The *captain* and the *sailors were* happy to be ashore.

  The *trees* and *shrubs need* more care.

- If the parts of a compound subject mean one and the same person or thing, the verb is singular; if the parts mean more than one, the verb is plural.

  The *secretary* and *treasurer is* not present. (one person)

  The *secretary* and the *treasurer are* not present. (more than one person)

- When *each* or *every* modify singular subjects joined by *and,* the verb is singular.

  Each *boy* and each *girl brings* a donation.

  Each *woman* and *man has asked* the same questions.

5. Alternative subjects—that is, subjects joined by *or, nor, either/or, neither/nor, not only/but also*—should be handled in the following manner:

- If the subjects are both singular, the verb is singular.

  Rosa or *Alicia* is responsible.

- If the subjects are plural, the verb is plural.

  Neither the *students* nor the *teachers were* impressed by his comments.

- If one of the subjects is singular and the other subject is plural, the verb agrees with the nearer subject.

  Either the Garcia *boys* or their *father goes* to the hospital each day.
  Either their *father* or the Garcia *boys go* to the hospital each day.

6. Collective nouns—*team, family, group, crew, gang, class, faculty,* and the like—take a singular verb if the verb is considered a unit but a plural verb if the group is considered as a number of individuals.

   The *team is playing* well tonight.
   The *team are getting* dressed. (Here the individuals are acting not as a unit but separately. If you don't like the way this sounds, rewrite as "The members of the team are getting dressed.")

7. Titles of books, essays, short stories, and plays; a word spoken of as a word; and the names of businesses take a singular verb.

   The Canterbury Tales was written by Geoffrey Chaucer.
   Markle Brothers has a sale this week.

8. Sums of money, distances, and measurements are followed by a singular verb when a unit is meant. They are followed by a plural verb when the individual elements are considered separately.

   Three dollars was the price. (unit)
   Three dollars were lying there. (individual)
   Five years is a long time. (unit)
   The *first five years were* difficult ones. (individual)

9. Be careful of agreement with nouns ending in *-s.* Several nouns ending in *-s* take a singular verb—for example, *aeronautics, civics, economics, ethics, measles, mumps.*

   Mumps is an extremely unpleasant disease.
   Economics is my major field of study.

10. Some nouns have only a plural form and so take only a plural verb—for example, *clothes, fireworks, scissors, pants, glasses.*

His *glasses are* dusty.
Mary's *clothes were* stylish and expensive.

Exercise 10 Making Subjects and Verbs Agree

Underline the verb that agrees in number with the subject.

1. "Two Kinds" (is, are) a short story by Amy Tan.

2. My pants (is, are) wrinkled.

3. Twenty pounds (is, are) a lot to lose in one month.

4. Physics (is, are) a difficult subject to master.

5. *60 Minutes* (is, are) a respected television program.

6. Sears (is, are) having a giant sale.

7. The scissors (is, are) very sharp.

8. Five miles (is, are) too far to walk.

9. The class (is, are) stretching their muscles.

10. My dog and my cat (is, are) sleeping on the couch.

Exercise 11 Making Subjects and Verbs Agree

Underline the verb that agrees in number with the subject.

1. Every year, New Orleans (is, are) the site of one of the longest and largest parties in the United States.

2. More than four million people from around the world (come, comes) to Mardi Gras, "the greatest free party on Earth."

3. Mardi Gras, which means "Fat Tuesday," (is, are) always forty-
   six days before Easter.

4. But twelve days before that, the crowd (begins, begin) to grow.

5. All of the bands in the state of Louisiana (converges, converge)
   on New Orleans.

6. A visitor, along with just about all of the city's residents,
   (enjoys, enjoy) nonstop jazz and blues music.

7. Cajun and Creole food (satisfies, satisfy) the revelers' hungry
   appetites.

8. There (is, are) about seventy parades, but the best ones (occurs,
   occur) during the last five days of the celebration.

9. Each of the spectacular parade floats (is, are) decorated and
   (carries, carry) riders wearing costumes.

10. Four miles (is, are) the length of a typical parade route.

11. Beads, coins, cups, and an occasional medallion (is, are) tossed
    from the floats into the crowd.

12. People who line the parade route (tries, try) to catch as many
    trinkets as they can.

13. One float, the best of all of that parade's floats, (wins, win) an
    award.

14. Some of the most popular festivities, besides a good parade, (is,
    are) the masked balls.

15. Every one of the costumes (is, are) outrageous and unique.

16. *Cajun Mardi Gras Masks* (is, are) a book that will give you some ideas.

17. All of the celebration (is, are) fun and interesting.

18. After dark, there (is, are) fireworks in the night sky.

19. Neither the participants nor the curious onlooker (wants, want) the party to end.

20. (Is, Are) these days of merrymaking something you'd enjoy?

✳ Consistency in Tense

Consider this statement:

> We went (1) downtown, and then we watch (2) a movie. Later we met (3) some friends from school, and we all go (4) to the mall. For most of the evening, we play (5) video games in arcades. It was (6) a typical but rather uneventful summer day.

Does the shifting verb tense bother you (to say nothing about the lack of development of ideas)? It should! The writer makes several unnecessary changes. Verbs 1, 3, and 6 are in the past tense, and verbs 2, 4, and 5 are in the present tense. Changing all verbs to past tense makes the statement much smoother.

> We went downtown, and then we watched a movie. Later we met some friends from school, and we all went to the mall. For most of the evening, we played video games in arcades. It was a typical but rather uneventful summer day.

In other instances you might want to maintain a consistent present tense. There are no inflexible rules about selecting a tense for a certain kind of writing, but you should be consistent, changing tense only for a good reason.

The present tense is customarily used in writing about literature, even if the literature was written long in the past:

> *Moby Dick* is a novel about Captain Ahab's obsession with a great white whale. Ahab *sets* sail with a full crew of sailors who *think* they *are going* on merely another whaling voyage. Most of the crew *are* experienced seamen.

The past tense is likely to serve you best in writing about your personal experiences and about historical events (although the present tense can often be used effectively to establish the feeling of intimacy and immediacy):

> In the summer of 1991, Hurricane Bob *hit* the Atlantic coast region. It *came* ashore near Cape Hatteras and *moved* north. The winds *reached* a speed of more than ninety miles per hour on Cape Cod but then *slackened* by the time Bob reached Maine.

Exercise 12   Making Verbs Consistent in Tense

Correct verbs as needed in the following paragraph to achieve verb-tense consistency. Most verbs will be present tense.

A trip to the dentist should not be a terrible experience—unless one goes to Dr. Litterfloss, credit dentist. Although he graduated *magna cum lately* from Ed's School of Dentistry, he had a reputation for being one of the dirtiest and most careless dentists in the state. He didn't even know about germs. He never used Novocain. He just spins the chair until his patients lost consciousness. Then he shot them with his x-ray gun from behind a lead wall. Sometimes he missed, and now his dental technician glows in the dark, so he didn't need a light as he worked. While drilling with one hand, he snacked on Vienna sausages with the other. Stray alley cats and mangy curs fought around his feet for food scraps, so he didn't need a cleaning service. He seldom washed his Black and Decker drill or Craftsman chisel, and he squirts tobacco juice into his spit sink. I recommended him only with strong reservation.

✳ Active and Passive Voice

Which of these sentences sounds better to you?

> Ken Griffey Jr. slammed a home run.
> A home run was slammed by Ken Griffey Jr.

Both sentences carry the same message, but the first expresses it more effectively. The subject (*Ken Griffey Jr.*) is the actor. The verb (*slammed*) is the action. The direct object (*home run*) is the receiver of the action. The second sentence lacks the vitality of the first because the receiver of the action is the subject; the doer is embedded in the prepositional phrase at the end of the sentence.

The first sentence demonstrates the active voice. It has an active verb (one that leads to a direct object), and the action moves from the beginning to the end of the sentence. The second exhibits the passive voice (with the action reflecting back on the subject). When given a choice, you should usually select the active voice. It promotes energy and directness.

The passive voice, though not usually the preferred form, does have its uses:

- When the doer of the action is unknown or unimportant

    My car was stolen. (The doer, a thief, is unknown.)

- When the receiver of the action is more important than the doer

    My neighbor was permanently disabled by an irresponsible drunk driver. (The neighbor's suffering is the focus, not the drunk driver.)

As you can see, the passive construction places the doer at the end of a prepositional phrase (as in the second example) or does not include the doer in the statement at all (as in the first example). Instead, the passive voice places the receiver of the action in the subject position, and it presents the verb in its past-tense form preceded by a *to be* helper. The transformation is a simple one:

ACTIVE	She read the book.
PASSIVE	The book was read by her.

Weak sentences often involve the unnecessary and ineffective use of the passive form; Exercise 13 concentrates on identifying the passive voice and changing it to active.

Exercise 13   Using Active and Passive Voice

Identify each sentence as either active voice (A) or passive voice (P) by writing A or P in the blank to the left. If a sentence with the passive form would be more effective in the active voice, rewrite it.

_____   1. A story will be told to you by me.

_____   2. A tragedy was experienced by a local ventriloquist the other day.

_____   3. Hundreds of his fans were being delighted by him at a local county fair performance.

_____   4. Suddenly his dummy burst into flames.

_____   5. Some speculated that spontaneous combustion caused the tragedy.

_____   6. However, the fire possibly was produced by
                          a system of cleverly placed mirrors engi-
                          neered by the ventriloquist to increase his
                          fame.

                          _____

                          _____

_____   7. The story was covered by all three major
                          television networks.

                          _____

                          _____

_____   8. The scene of the mysterious combustion
                          was viewed by thousands of curious folk.

                          _____

                          _____

_____   9. The ventriloquist has been made a rich man
                          by the publicity.

                          _____

                          _____

_____   10. In fact, he has been given several offers to
                          appear on television talk shows to discuss
                          the event.

                          _____

                          _____

_____   11. He lives happily with his new wealth, but he
                          will never forget how his little wooden
                          friend and their friendship went up in
                          smoke.

                          _____

                          _____

✳ Strong Verbs

Because the verb is an extremely important part of any sentence, it should be chosen with care. Some of the most widely used verbs are the *being* verbs: *is, was, were, are, am.* We couldn't get along in English without them, but writers often use them when more forceful and effective verbs are available.

Consider these examples:

WEAK VERB	He *is* the leader of the people.
STRONG VERB	He *leads* the people.
WEAK VERB	She *was* the first to finish.
STRONG VERB	She *finished* first.

▌Exercise 14 ▌ Using Strong Verbs

Replace the weak verbs with stronger ones in the following sentences. Delete unnecessary words to make each sentence even more concise if you can.

1. My watch is running slowly.

2. My computer is quite inexpensive.

3. The horse was a fast runner.

4. They were writers who wrote well.

5. The dog is sleeping on the bed.

6. Mr. Hawkins is a real estate salesperson.

7. José is in attendance at Santa Ana College.

8. This assignment is something I like.

9. We are the successful students here.

10. She is in the process of combing her hair.

Exercise 15 Using Strong Verbs

Replace the weak verbs with stronger ones in the following sentences. Delete unnecessary words to make each sentence even more concise if you can.

1. Babe Ruth was the hitter of many home runs.

2. The chef was a man with a fondness for food.

3. To graduate in two years is my plan.

4. John Hancock was the first signer of the Declaration of Independence.

5. Juanita is the organizer of the event.

6. Cooking is something she likes to do.

7. Carl was the owner of the restaurant.

8. Tiger Woods will be the winner of the tournament.

9. They were in love with each other.

10. His passion for her was in a state of demise.

✳ Chapter Review

Exercise 16 Correcting Verb Problems

Correct problems with verb form, tense, agreement, strength, and voice. As a summary of a novel, this piece should be mostly in the present tense.

Summary of *The Old Man and the Sea*

Santiago, one of many local fishermen, have not caught a fish in eighty-four days. Young Manolin, despite the objections of his parents, has a belief in the old man. His parents says Santiago is unlucky, and they will not let their son go fishing with him.

The next day Santiago sit sail. Soon he catch a small tuna, which he used for bait. Then a huge marlin hit the bait with a strike. The old man cannot rise the fish to the surface, and it pulled the boat throughout the rest of the day and during the night.

During the second day, Santiago's hand is injured by the line and he become extremely tired, but he holds on. When the fish moves to the surface, Santiago notes that it was two feet longer than his skiff. It is the biggest fish he has ever saw. He thinks in wonder if he will be up to the task of catching it. With the line braced across his shoulders, he sleeped for a while. As he dreams gloriously of lions and porpoises and of being young, he is awaken by the fish breaking water again, and Santiago is sure the fish is tiring. He lays in the boat and waits.

On the third day, the fish came to the surface. Santiago pull steadily on the line, and finally it is harpooned and killed by Santiago. The fish is tied to the skiff by him. But sharks attacked and mutilate the huge marlin. Using an oar, he beats on the sharks courageously with all his strength, but they strips the fish to a skeleton.

With the bones still tied to the skiff, the exhausted old man returned to shore. Other fishermen and tourists marvel at the eighteen-foot skeleton of the fish as the old man lays asleep. The young boy knew he has much to learn from the old man and is determined to go fishing with him.

Exercise 17 Writing Sentences with Correct Verbs

Each of the following verbs appears in its base form. Change the verb form to the tense specified in parentheses and include it in a sentence of ten or more words. (See pages 85–88 for verb forms.)

1. *eat* (to past tense) _____

_____

2. *begin* (to future) _____

_____

3. *see* (to past perfect) _____

_____

4. *walk* (to future perfect) _____

_____

5. *speak* (to present perfect) _____

_____

6. *go* (to future progressive) _____

_____

7. *drink* (to present progressive) _____

_____

8. *dance* (to past progressive) _____

_____

9. *flew* (to present perfect progressive) _____

_____

10. *grow* (to past perfect progressive)_____

_____

11. *choose* (to future perfect progressive)_____

_____

Pronouns

Should you say, "Between you and *I*" or "Between you and *me*"? What about "Let's you and *I* do this" or "Let's you and *me* do this"? Are you confused about when to use *who* and *whom*? Is it "Everyone should wear *their* coat, or *his* coat, or *his or her* coat"? Is there anything wrong with saying, "When *you* walk down the streets of Laredo"?

The examples in the first paragraph represent the most common problems people have with pronouns. This chapter will help you identify the standard forms and understand why they are correct. The result should be expertise and confidence.

※ Pronoun Case

Case is the form a pronoun takes as it fills a position in a sentence. Words such as *you* and *it* do not change, but others do, and they change in predictable ways. For example, *I* is a subject word and *me* is an object word. As you refer to yourself, you will select a pronoun that fits a certain part of sentence structure. You say, "*I* will write the paper," not "*Me* will write the paper," because *I* is in the subject position. But you say, "She will give the apple to *me*," not "She will give the apple to *I*" because *me* is in the object position. These are pronouns that do change:

Subject	Object
I	me
he	him
she	her
we	us
they	them
who	whom, whomever

Subjective Case

Person	Singular	Plural
First	I	we
Second	you	you
Third	he she it	they
	who	

Subjective pronouns can fill two positions in a sentence.

1. Pronouns in the subjective case may fill subject positions.
   a. Some will be easy to identify because they are at the beginning of the sentence.

   I dance in the park.

   He dances in the park.

   She dances in the park.

   We dance in the park.

   They dance in the park.

   Who is dancing in the park?

   b. Others will be more difficult to identify because they are not at the beginning of a sentence and may not appear to be part of a clause. The words *than* and *as* are signals for these special arrangements, which can be called incompletely stated clauses.

   He is taller than *I* (am).

   She is younger than *we* (are).

   We work as hard as *they* (do).

   The words *am, are,* and *do,* which complete the clauses, have been omitted. We are actually saying, "He is taller than *I am,*" "She is younger than *we are,*" and "We work as hard as *they do.*" The italicized pronouns are subjects of "understood" verbs.

2. Pronouns in the subjective case may refer back to the subject.
   a. They may follow a form of the verb *to be*, such as *was, were, are, am,* and *is.*

   I believe it is *he.*

   It was *she* who spoke.

   The victims were *they.*

   b. Some nouns and pronouns refer back to an earlier noun without referring back through the verb.

   The leading candidates—Juan, Darnelle, Steve, Kimlieu, and *I*—made speeches.

Objective Case

Person	Singular	Plural
First	me	us
Second	you	you
Third	him her it	them
	whom	

Objective pronouns can also fill two positions in sentences.

1. Pronouns in the objective case may fill object positions.
   a. They may be objects after the verb. A direct object answers the question *what?* or *whom?* in connection with the verb.

   We brought *it* to your house. (*What* did we bring? *it*)

   We saw *her* in the library (*Whom* did we see? *her*)

   An indirect object answers the question *to whom* in connection with the verb.

   I gave *him* the message. (*To whom* did I give the message? *to him*)

   The doctor told *us* the test results. (*To whom* did the doctor tell the results? *to us*)

b. They may be objects after prepositions.

> The problem was clear to *us*.
>
> I offered the opportunity to Steve and *him*.

2. Object pronouns may also refer back to object words.

> They gave the results to us—Judy and *me*.
>
> The judge addressed the defendants—John and *her*.

Techniques for Determining Case

Here are three techniques that will help you decide which pronoun to use when the choice seems difficult:

1. If you have a compound element (such as a subject or an object of a preposition), consider only the pronoun part. The sound alone will probably tell you the answer.

> She gave the answer to Marie and (I, me).

Marie and the pronoun make up a compound object of the preposition *to*. Disregard the noun, *Marie*, and ask yourself, "Would I say, 'She gave the answer *to me* or *to I*'?" The way the words sound would tell you the answer is *to me*. Of course, if you immediately notice that the pronoun is in an object position, you need not bother with sound.

2. If you are choosing between *who* (subject word) and *whom* (object word), look to the right to see if the next verb has a subject. If it does not, the pronoun probably *is* the subject, but if it does, the pronoun probably is an object.

A related technique works the same way. If the next important word after *who* or *whom* in a statement is a noun or pronoun, the correct word will usually be *whom*. However, if the next important word is not a noun or pronoun, the correct word will be *who*.

To apply these techniques, you must disregard qualifier clauses such as "I think," "it seems," and "we hope."

> The person (*who*, whom) works hardest will win. (*Who* is the correct answer because it is the subject of the verb *works*.)
>
> The person (who, *whom*) we admire most is José. (*Whom* is the correct answer because the next verb, *admire*, already has a subject, *we*. *Whom* is an object.)

Tom is the person (*who*, whom), we hope, has won. (*We hope* is a qualifier clause, so we disregard it. Because we need a subject for the verb *has won*, we select the subject word *who*.)

3. *Let's* is made up of the words *let* and *us* and means "you *let us*"; therefore, when you select a pronoun to follow it, consider the two original words and select another object word—*me*.

> Let's you and (I, *me*) take a trip to Westwood. (Think of "You let us, you and me, take a trip to Westwood." *Us* and *me* are object words.)

Exercise 1 Selecting Pronouns

Underline the correct pronouns.

1. We admired his beer can collection, so he left it to (I, me) and (she, her) in his will.

2. (He, Him) and (I, me) found true love via the Lovers-R-Us.com online dating service.

3. He deserves to win more than (her, she).

4. The final showdown will be between (they, them) and (we, us).

5. No one can beat (we, us), so let's you and (I, me) apply to be contestants on the *Wheel of Fortune* game show.

6. (Us, We) attorneys resent being compared to sharks.

7. The show delighted and amazed (us, we) puppet enthusiasts.

8. The individual (who, whom) gave his mother a vacuum cleaner for Mother's Day deserves a lump of coal for Christmas.

9. You can hire (whoever, whomever) you choose.

10. Between you and (I, me), I didn't care for the twenty-minute

    drum solo.

Exercise 2 Selecting Pronouns

Underline the correct pronouns.

1. (She, Her) and (I, me) went to the Ripley's Believe It or Not

   Museum.

2. (We, Us) young people are fascinated by the weird, the gross,

   and the creepy.

3. I would rather go to the museum with you than with (she, her).

4. There are those (who, whom) would urge you not to waste your

   money to see oddities like shrunken heads and a portrait of

   John Wayne made of dryer lint.

5. Robert L. Ripley, an eccentric newspaper cartoonist (who,

   whom) loved to travel, collected strange things.

6. He is the man (who, whom) we can thank for acquiring many

   of the artifacts now housed in forty-four "Odditoriums" in ten

   different countries.

7. (Who, Whom) wouldn't be entertained by a stuffed six-legged

   cow or pictures of two-headed lambs and other freaks of nature?

8. And don't forget the bizarre videos, like the one of a man (who, whom) swallows and then regurgitates a live mouse.

9. I feel sorry for (whoever, whomever) misses the replica of the "Mona Lisa" made out of croutons.

10. Just between you and (I, me), though, the wax figures of bizarre accident victims, like the man impaled on a crowbar, were a little unnerving.

Exercise 3 Selecting Pronouns

Underline the correct pronouns.

1. Let's you and (I, me) consider some stories called urban legends.

2. These are stories heard by people like you and (I, me), which are passed on as if they were true.

3. We hear them from people (who, whom) have heard them from others.

4. You have probably heard more of them than (I, me), but I'll tell some anyway.

5. One is about a guard dog named Gork (who, whom) was found choking in his owner's bedroom.

6. The owner, (who, whom) loved Gork dearly, took him to the veterinarian, left him, and headed home.

7. While driving home, the owner answered his cell phone, asking

   "To (who, whom) am I speaking?"

8. "This is your vet calling. Just between you and (I, me), you

   have a big problem here."

9. "Gork has someone's detached finger stuck in his throat, and

   I've called the police, (who, whom) are on their way to your

   house."

10. Eventually the police arrested an angry armed man (who,

    whom) they suspected had broken into the owner's house,

    where Gork had bitten off and choked on the intruder's finger

    while the intruder, (who, whom) had crawled into a closet,

    passed out from loss of blood.

Exercise 4 Selecting Pronouns

Underline the correct pronouns.

1. Another famous urban legend, involving two motorists, was

   told to my sister and (me, I) years ago.

2. Between you and (I, me), the story is sexist, but this is the way

   (we, us) heard it.

3. A motorist, (who, whom) was named Al, needed someone to

   push his car, so he called on Sue, his neighbor, (who, whom)

   lived next door.

4. "I need a push to get my car started," he said to her. "Let's you and (I, me) work together, and I'll be grateful forever."

5. "You're a special person (who, whom) I've always wanted to befriend," she said happily. "Tell me what to do."

6. "My car has an automatic transmission, which means the car won't start at less than thirty-five miles per hour," said Al, (who, whom) talked fast.

7. Al sat in his car as happy as (her, she) when he looked in his rear-view mirror and saw (she, her) heading toward his back bumper at a high speed.

8. After the collision, Al stumbled out of his car and confronted Sue, (who, whom), despite her injuries, was smiling.

9. "Look what you've done to you and (I, me)!" Al yelled.

10. "Let's you and (I, me) review what you said," she answered coolly. "You said, 'thirty-five miles per hour,' and that's exactly what I was doing."

✳ Pronoun-Antecedent Agreement

Every pronoun refers to an earlier noun, the **antecedent** of the pronoun, which is the noun that the pronoun replaces. The pronoun brings the reader back to the earlier thought. Here are some examples:

> I tried to buy *tickets* for the concert, but *they* were all sold.
> *Roger* painted a picture of a pickup truck. *It* was so good that *he* entered *it* in an art show.

A pronoun agrees with its antecedent in person, number, and gender. **Person**—first, second, or third—indicates perspective, or point of view. **Number** indicates singular or plural. **Gender** indicates sex: masculine, feminine, or neuter.

Subject Words			*Object Words*		
Person	**Singular**	**Plural**	**Person**	**Singular**	**Plural**
First	I	we	**First**	me	us
Second	you	you	**Second**	you	you
Third	he, she, it	they	**Third**	him, her, it	them

Agreement in Person

Avoid needless shifting in person, which means shifting of point of view, such as from *I* to *you*. The following paragraph is an example of an inconsistent point of view. See if you can tell where the shifts occur.

INCONSISTENT   The wedding did not go well. It was a disaster. *You* could see the trouble develop when the caterers started serving drinks before the ceremony. Then the bride started arguing with her future mother-in-law. *I* was ready to leave right away. After that, the sound system went out and the band canceled. *You* wished *you* hadn't come, but *you* had to stay. *I* will never forget that day.

The word *you* is second-person point of view; the word *I* is first person. When the writer switches back and forth, the result is reader confusion and annoyance. The following revision corrects the problem by making the point of view consistently first person.

CONSISTENT   The wedding did not go well. It was a disaster. *I* could see the trouble develop when the caterers started serving drinks before the ceremony. Then the bride started arguing with her future mother-in-law. *I* was ready to leave right away. After that, the sound system went out and the band canceled. *I* wished *I* hadn't come, but *I* had to stay. *I* will never forget that day.

Agreement in Number

Most problems with pronoun-antecedent agreement involve number. The principles are simple: If the antecedent (the word the pronoun refers back to) is singular, use a singular pronoun. If the antecedent is plural, use a plural pronoun.

1. A singular antecedent requires a singular pronoun.

   Jim forgot *his* notebook.

2. A plural antecedent requires a plural pronoun.

   Many *students* cast *their* votes today.

3. A singular indefinite pronoun as an antecedent takes a singular pronoun. Most indefinite pronouns are singular. The following are common indefinite singular pronouns: *anybody, anyone, each, either, everybody, everyone, no one, nobody, one, somebody, someone.*

   Each of the girls brought *her* book.

4. A plural indefinite pronoun as an antecedent takes a plural pronoun.

   Few knew *their* assignments.

5. Certain indefinite pronouns do not clearly express either a singular or plural number. Agreement, therefore, depends on the meaning of the sentence. These pronouns are *all, any, none,* and *some.*

   All of the melon *was* good.

   All of the melons *were* good.

   None of the pie *is* acceptable.

   None of the pies *are* acceptable.

6. Two or more antecedents, singular or plural, take a plural pronoun. Such antecedents are usually joined by *and* or by commas and *and.*

   Howard and his *parents* bought *their* presents early.

   The *players, team owner,* and *fans* expressed *their* views.

7. Alternate antecedents—that is, antecedents joined by *or, nor, whether/or, either/or, neither/nor, not only/but also*—require a pronoun that agrees with the nearer antecedent.

Neither John nor his *friends* lost *their* way.

Neither his friends nor *John* lost *his* way.

8. In a sentence with the expression *one of*, the antecedent is usually the plural noun that follows.

    He is one of those *people who* want *their* money now.

9. In a sentence with the expression *only one of*, the antecedent is usually the singular word *one*.

    She is the only *one of* the members *who* wants *her* money now.

10. When collective nouns such as *team, jury, committee*, and *band* are used as antecedents, they take a singular pronoun if they are considered as units.

    The *jury* is doing *its* [not *their*] best.

    When individual behavior is suggested, collective nouns take a plural form.

    The *jury* are putting on *their* coats.

11. The words *each, every*, and *many a(n)* before a noun make the noun singular.

    Each child and *adult* was *his* or *her* own authority.

    Each and *every person* doubted *himself* or *herself*.

    Many a person is capable of knowing *himself* or *herself*.

Agreement in Gender

The pronoun should agree with its antecedent in gender, if the gender of the antecedent is specific. Masculine and feminine pronouns are gender-specific: *he, him, she, her*. Others are neuter: *I, we, me, us, it, they, them, who, whom, that, which*. The words *who* and *whom* refer to people. *That* can refer to ideas, things, and people, but usually not to people. *Which* refers to ideas and things, but never to people.

My *girlfriend* gave me *her* best advice. (feminine)

Mighty *Casey* tried *his* best. (masculine)

The *people with whom* I work are loud. (neuter)

Indefinite singular pronouns used as antecedents require, of course, singular pronouns. Handling the gender of these singular pronouns is not as obvious; opinion is divided.

1. Traditionally, writers have used the masculine form of pronouns to refer to the indefinite singular pronouns when the gender is unknown.

   Everyone should work until *he* drops.

2. The use of the masculine form of pronouns alone, however, suggests a sex bias. To avoid a perceived sex bias, most writers prefer to use *he or she* or *his or her* instead of just *he* or *his*.

   Everyone should work until *he or she* drops.

3. Although option 1 is less cumbersome, it is illogical to many listeners and readers, and option 2 used several times in a short passage can be awkward. To avoid those possible problems, writers often use plural forms.

   All people should work until *they* drop.

In any case, avoid using a plural pronoun with a singular indefinite pronoun; such usage violates the basic principle of number agreement.

   INCORRECT   *Everyone* should do *their* best.

Exercise 5 Selecting Pronouns: Person, Gender, and Number

Correct the faulty use of pronouns for problems in person, gender, and number.

1. People fishing on the Amazon River know that when you hook a bloodthirsty piranha, you have to be careful of its razor-sharp teeth.

2. Most people know that you can make it rain by washing your car.

3. Americans may have no idea where Peru is located, but you still know the words to all of the Bee Gees' songs.

4. I got her to admit that astrology is hooey, but you couldn't

   convince her to stop reading her daily horoscope.

5. Every male knows that you will never hear a woman laugh at

   the antics of the Three Stooges.

6. She knew that the seating-chart mistake was her fault because

   you should not place a baron above a count.

7. The magicians forgot that you can't fool everyone all of the

   time.

8. Wise people remind us that if you don't know history, you are

   doomed to repeat it.

9. They should have known that you can't keep a good woman

   down.

10. Pyromaniac chefs love to flambé, especially when you light the

    Baked Alaska on fire.

Exercise 6 Selecting Pronouns: Person, Gender, and Number

Underline the correct pronoun for gender and number.

1. The fry cooks at Campus Kitchen have developed a new

   chocolate cookie that (they, he or she) will try to sell to (us, we)

   students.

2. The cookies taste terrible, but an official EPA test proved that

   (they, it) are biodegradable.

3. The weather forecasters were especially pleased when (their, his or her) prediction for tornadoes was accurate.

4. Commuters driving home in (their, his or her) cars can learn to swear in several tongues by listening to foreign language tapes.

5. My neighbors avoid harmful radiation by wearing (his or her, their) lead suits.

6. If all class members would work together, (they, he or she) might accomplish great things.

7. The snake-handling troupe brought (their, its) defanged rattlesnakes to show the curious children.

8. In one day, a hummingbird can eat (its, their) weight in nectar.

9. Each member of the Boffo Brothers acrobatic troupe can balance a lawn chair on (his, their) nose.

10. Those wacky acrobats will expand (its, their) act to table balancing next year.

✳ Pronoun Reference

A pronoun must refer clearly to its antecedent. Because a pronoun is a substitute word, it can express meaning clearly and definitely only if its antecedent is easily identified.

In some sentence constructions, gender and number make the reference clear.

> Thomas and Jane discussed *his* absences and *her* good attendance. (gender)
>
> If the three older boys in the *club* carry out those plans, *it* will break up. (number)

Avoid ambiguous reference. The following sentences illustrate the kind of confusion that results from structuring sentences with more than one possible antecedent for the pronoun.

UNCLEAR	John gave David *his* money and clothes.
CLEAR	John gave his own money and clothes to David.

UNCLEAR	Mary told her sister that *her* car had a flat tire.
CLEAR	Mary said to her sister, "Your car has a flat tire."

When using a pronoun to refer to a general idea, make sure that the reference is clear. The pronouns used frequently in this way are *this, that, which,* and *it.* The best solution may be to recast the sentence to omit the pronoun in question.

UNCLEAR	She whistled the same tune over and over, *which* irritated me.
CLEAR	She whistled the same tune over and over, a *habit* that irritated me.
RECAST	Her whistling the same tune over and over irritated me.

Exercise 7 Selecting Pronouns: Reference and Agreement

Correct the problems in pronoun reference and agreement.

1. I eat fast food only three times a week, which is un-American of me.

2. The supervisors told the staff members that they would be getting a big raise.

3. If a woman is looking for quality men, you should log on to www.select-a-hunk.com.

4. She called to find out the store's hours, but they didn't answer.

5. When he smashed into the pyramid of cat food with his shopping cart, it was destroyed.

6. It says in the newspaper that an elephant is on the loose.

7. I tend to submit my assignments late, which hurts my grade.

8. The Great Oz told the Tin Man that he already possessed the
   thing he craved most.

9. They say that the horse named Cheese Whiz may win the
   Triple Crown.

10. Spiderman told Superman that he may have given up on love
    too soon.

✳ **Chapter Review**

Exercise 8 Writing Sentences with Correct Pronouns

*Write a sentence using each of the following words. Do not use
the word as the first one in the sentence. One sentence should
contain the word* between *before a pronoun such as "between you
and* _____.*"*

1. she _____

   _____

   _____

2. her _____

   _____

   _____

3. him _____

   _____

   _____

4. us _____

_____

_____

5. who _____

_____

_____

6. whom _____

_____

_____

7. me _____

_____

_____

8. I _____

_____

_____

9. they _____

_____

_____

10. them _____

_____

_____

Adjectives and Adverbs

Adjectives modify (describe) nouns and pronouns and answer the questions *Which one? What kind?* and *How many?*

WHICH ONE?   The <u>new</u> <u>car</u> is mine.
              adj   n

WHAT KIND?   <u>Mexican</u> <u>food</u> is my favorite.
             adj   n

HOW MANY?   A <u>few</u> <u>friends</u> are all one needs.
              adj   n

Adverbs modify verbs, adjectives, or other adverbs and answer the questions *How? Where? When?* and *To what degree?* Most words ending in *-ly* are adverbs.

WHERE?   The cuckoo <u>flew</u> <u>south</u>.
                    v   adv

WHEN?   The cuckoo <u>flew</u> <u>yesterday</u>.
                   v   adv

WHY?   The cuckoo <u>flew</u> <u>because of the cold weather</u>.
                  v   adv phrase

HOW?   The cuckoo <u>flew</u> <u>swiftly</u>.
                  v   adv

<u>Without adjectives and</u> <u>adverbs,</u> <u>even</u> John Steinbeck, the <u>famous</u>
        adv phrase   adv   adj

<u>Nobel Prize–winning</u> author, <u>surely</u> could <u>not</u> have described the
        adj   adv   adv

<u>crafty</u> octopus <u>very</u> <u>well</u>.
  adj   adv   adv

Exercise 1   Using Adjectives and Adverbs

The following excerpt is from Steinbeck's novel Cannery Row. *Fill in the blanks for the adjectives and adverbs that have been omitted.*

(1) _____ the (2) _____ murderer, the octopus, steals

(3) _____, (4) _____, (5) _____, moving like a

(6) _____ mist, pretending (7) _____ to be a bit of weed,

(8) _____ a rock, (9) _____ a lump of (10) _____

meat while its (11) _____ eyes watch (12) _____. It

oozes and flows toward a (13) _____ crab, and as it comes close

its (14) _____ eyes burn and its body turns (15) _____

with the (16) _____ color of anticipation and rage.

(17) _____ (18) _____ it runs (19) _____ on the

tips of its arms, as (20) _____ as a (21) _____ cat. It

leaps (22) _____ on the crab, there is a puff of

(23) _____ fluid, and the (24) _____ mass is obscured in

the (25) _____ cloud while the octopus murders the crab.

Of course, Steinbeck vividly depicts his subject through his skillful choice of nouns such as *murderer* and *rage,* and of verbs such as *steals, oozes, flows, burn, runs,* and *leaps,* but the absence of adjectives and adverbs eliminates a whole dimension of expression.

The missing adjectives and adverbs are the following: (1) Then, (2) creeping, (3) out, (4) slowly, (5) softly, (6) gray, (7) now, (8) now, (9) now, (10) decaying, (11) evil, (12) coldly, (13) feeding, (14) yellow, (15) rosy, (16) pulsing, (17) Then, (18) suddenly, (19) lightly, (20) ferociously, (21) charging, (22) savagely, (23) black, (24) struggling, (25) sepia.

We have two concerns regarding the use of adjectives and adverbs in writing. One is a matter of diction, or word choice—in this case, selecting adjectives and adverbs that will strengthen the writing. The other is how to identify and correct problems with modifiers.

✳ Selecting Adjectives and Adverbs

If you want to finish the sentence "She danced _____," you have many adverbs to select from, including these:

bewitchingly	angelically	quaintly	zestfully
gracefully	grotesquely	carnally	smoothly
divinely	picturesquely	serenely	unevenly

If you want to finish the sentence "She was a(n) _____ speaker," you have another large selection, this time of adjectives such as the following:

distinguished	dependable	effective	sly
influential	impressive	polished	astute
adequate	boring	abrasive	humorous

Adjectives and adverbs can be used to enhance communication. If you have a thought, you know what it is, but when you deliver that thought to someone else, you may not say or write what you mean. Your thought may be eloquent and your word choice weak. Keep in mind that no two words mean exactly the same thing. Further, some words are vague or general. If you settle for a common word such as *good* or a slang word such as *neat* to characterize something that you like, you will be limiting your communication. Of course, those who know you best may understand fairly well; after all, certain people who are really close may be able to convey ideas using only grunts and gestures.

But what if you want to write to someone you hardly know to explain how you feel about an important issue? Then the more precise the word, the better the communication. By using modifiers you may be able to add significant information. Anything can be overdone, however, so use adjectives and adverbs wisely and economically.

Your first resource in searching for more effective adjectives should be your own vocabulary storehouse. Another resource is a good thesaurus (book of synonyms). Finally, you may want to collaborate with others to discuss and share ideas.

Exercise 2 Using Adjectives

Provide adjectives to modify these nouns, using a dictionary, a the-saurus, or the resources designated by your instructor. Use only single words, not adjective phrases.

1. A(n) _____ dog ignored the cat.

2. A(n) _____ comedian waited for applause.

3. A(n) _____ voice cried out in the night.

4. A(n) _____ neighbor turned up his boom box.

5. A(n) _____ ballplayer never gives up.

6. A(n) _____ party occurs only in one's imagination.

7. A(n) _____ singer sang off key.

8. A(n) _____ date waited at the club.

9. A(n) _____ car careened down the street.

10. A(n) _____ job is hard to find.

Exercise 3 Using Adverbs

Provide adverbs to modify these verbs, using a dictionary, a the-saurus, or the resources designated by your instructor. Use only single words, not adverb phrases.

1. Write _____ and clearly.

2. Run _____ and get help.

3. Talk _____ and carry a big stick.

4. Walk _____ and think fast.

5. Marry _____ and suffer at leisure.

6. Smile _____ at your boss.

7. Drive _____ and carefully.

8. Leave _____ and forget my name.

9. Laugh _____ at adversity.

10. Study _____ and get smart.

✳ Comparative and Superlative Forms

For making comparisons, most adjectives and adverbs have three different forms: the positive (one), the comparative (two), and the superlative (three or more).

Adjectives

1. Some adjectives follow a regular pattern:

Positive (one)	Comparative (two)	Superlative (three or more)
nice	nicer	nicest
rich	richer	richest
big	bigger	biggest
tall	taller	tallest
lonely	lonelier	loneliest
terrible	more terrible	most terrible
beautiful	more beautiful	most beautiful

These are usually the rules:

a. Add -er to short adjectives (one or two syllables) to rank units of two:

Julian is *nicer* than Sam.

b. Add -est to short adjectives (one or two syllables) to rank units of three or more:

Of the fifty people I know, Julian is the *kindest*.

c. Add the word *more* to long adjectives (three or more syllables) to rank units of two.

My hometown is *more beautiful* than yours.

d. Add the word *most* to long adjectives (three or more syllables) to rank units of three or more.

My hometown is the *most beautiful* in all America.

2. Some adjectives are irregular in the way they change to show comparison.

Positive (one)	Comparative (two)	Superlative (three or more)
good	better	best
bad	worse	worst

Adverbs

1. For most adverbs, use the word *more* before the comparative form (two) and the word *most* before the superlative form (three or more).

> Joan performed *skillfully.* (modifier)
>
> Jim performed *more skillfully* than Joan. (comparative modifier)
>
> But Tom performed *most skillfully* of all. (superlative modifier)

2. Avoid double negatives. Words such as *no, not, none, nothing, never, hardly, barely,* and *scarcely* should not be combined.

> DOUBLE NEGATIVE   I do *not* have *no* time for recreation. (incorrect)
>
> SINGLE NEGATIVE   I have *no* time for recreation. (correct)
>
> DOUBLE NEGATIVE   I've *hardly never* lied. (incorrect)
>
> SINGLE NEGATIVE   I've *hardly* ever lied. (correct)

3. Do not confuse adjectives with adverbs. Among the most commonly confused adjectives and adverbs are *good/well, bad/badly,* and *real/really.* The words *good, bad,* and *real* are always adjectives. *Well* is sometimes an adjective. The words *badly* and *really* are always adverbs. *Well* is usually an adverb.

    To distinguish these words, consider what is being modified. Remember that adjectives modify nouns and pronouns and that adverbs modify verbs, adjectives, and other adverbs.

> WRONG   I feel *badly* today. (We're concerned with the condition of *I.*)
>
> RIGHT   I feel *bad* today. (The adjective *bad* modifies the pronoun *I.*)
>
> WRONG   She feels *well* about that choice. (We're concerned with the condition of *she.*)
>
> RIGHT   She feels *good* about that choice. (The adjective *good* modifies the pronoun *she.*)
>
> WRONG   Ted plays the piano *good.* (The adjective *good* modifies the verb *plays,* but adjectives should not modify verbs.)
>
> RIGHT   Ted plays the piano *well.* (The adverb *well* modifies the verb *plays.*)
>
> WRONG   He did *real* well. (Here the adjective *real* modifies the adverb *well,* but adjectives should not modify adverbs.)

RIGHT   He did *really* well. (The adverb *really* modifies the adverb *well*.)

4. Do not use an adverb such as *very, more,* or *most* before adjectives such as *perfect, round, unique, square,* and *straight*.

WRONG   It is more round.

RIGHT   It is round.

RIGHT   It is more nearly round.

Exercise 4 Selecting Adjectives and Adverbs

Underline the correct word or words.

1. Betty Skelton was one of the (most, more) successful female stunt pilots of the 1940s and 1950s.

2. In the 1930s and 1940s, the public was (real, really) interested in watching acrobatic air shows.

3. Skelton was (not hardly, hardly) going to sit there and watch the men have all the fun.

4. She wanted (bad, badly) to learn to fly, and she was (real, really) adventurous, so she learned to perform daredevil feats.

5. Her small, agile airplane, which was named Little Stinker, performed tricks (well, good).

6. One of her (better, best) stunts was the inverted ribbon cut.

7. It was a (real, really) thrill to watch her fly upside down twelve feet off the ground and use her propeller to slice a foil strip strung between two poles.

8. The crowd could (not hardly, hardly) contain its excitement.

9. She earned only $25 for each air show, so the pay was (bad, badly).

10. But according to Betty, her six-year acrobatic flying career was the (more, most) fun time in her life.

Exercise 5 Using Adjectives and Adverbs

Correct any problems with adjectives and adverbs in the following sentences.

1. Today, in the twenty-first century, dressing like 1960s hippies is a real big trend for many young people.

2. There are some signs that the 1970s, when fashion has never been worser, is next.

3. Women are already stomping around in the most biggest platform shoes I've ever seen.

4. I do not have no regrets about wearing a lot of polyester in the 1970s.

5. But we can only pray that powder-blue leisure suits with wide lapels don't never come back into style.

6. Men thought they looked real suave when they wore these suits with shirts unbuttoned to show their chest hair and gold chains.

7. The male disco dancer thought he could dance especially good in white gabardine pants like the ones John Travolta wore in *Saturday Night Fever*.

8. In the 1970s, a very unique look was achieved with fashions like knee-high glitter socks and hats made out of beer cans crocheted together.

9. Women thought they looked well in knee-length corduroy gaucho pants and dingo boots.

10. Was there never no sillier piece of jewelry than the mood ring?

Exercise 6 Selecting Adjectives and Adverbs

Underline the correct word or words.

1. In the early 1900s, if you were (real, really) (good, well) at tug-of-war, you could have competed in the Olympics.

2. Tug-of-war used to be an Olympic sport, but it's not (no, any) more.

3. I can (not, not hardly) believe that sports like golf and croquet used to be part of the Olympic Games, too.

4. Today, one of the (odder, oddest) of all of the Olympic sports is curling.

5. No, it's not a competition to see which hairdresser can create the (more, most) beautiful style.

6. And curling enthusiasts get (real, really) angry if you compare their sport to shuffleboard on ice.

7. But when people see curlers sweeping the ice with brooms to help a 42-pound rock glide better, they often conclude that the sport is one of the (stranger, strangest) they've ever seen.

8. Another odd Olympic sport is for those who can ski and shoot rifles (good, well).

9. In the biathlon, the athlete who takes home the gold is the one who hits targets (best, better) and skis (faster, fastest).

10. The triathlon combines swimming, cycling, and running, but a blend of cross-country skiing and marksmanship seems (more, most) odd.

✳ Dangling and Misplaced Modifiers

Modifiers should clearly relate to the word or words they modify.

1. A modifier that gives information but doesn't refer to a word or group of words already in the sentence is called a **dangling modifier.**

> DANGLING *Walking down the street,* a snake startled him. (Who was walking down the street? The person isn't mentioned in the sentence.)
>
> CORRECT *Walking down the street, Don* was startled by a snake.
>
> CORRECT As *Don* walked down the street, *he* was startled by a snake.

DANGLING *At the age of six,* my uncle died. (Who was six years old? The person isn't mentioned in the modifier.)

CORRECT *When I was six,* my uncle died.

2. A modifier that is placed so that it modifies the wrong word or words is called a **misplaced modifier.** The term also applies to words that are positioned to unnecessarily divide closely related parts of sentences such as infinitives (*to* plus verb) or subjects and verbs.

MISPLACED The sick man went to a doctor *with a high fever.*

CORRECT The sick man *with a high fever* went to a doctor.

MISPLACED I saw a great movie *sitting in my pickup.*

CORRECT *Sitting in my pickup,* I saw a great movie.

MISPLACED Kim found many new graves *walking through the cemetery.*

CORRECT *Walking through the cemetery,* Kim found many new graves.

MISPLACED I forgot all about my sick dog *kissing my girlfriend.*

CORRECT *Kissing my girlfriend,* I forgot all about my sick dog.

MISPLACED They tried to *earnestly and sincerely* complete the task. (splitting of the infinitive *to complete*)

CORRECT They tried *earnestly and sincerely* to complete the task.

MISPLACED My neighbor, *while walking to the store,* was mugged. (unnecessarily dividing the subject and verb)

CORRECT *While walking to the store,* my neighbor was mugged.

Try this procedure in working with the following exercises.

1. Circle the modifier.
2. Draw an arrow from the modifier to the word or words it modifies.
3. If the modifier does not relate directly to anything in the sentence, it is dangling, and you must recast the sentence.
4. If the modifier does not modify the nearest word or words, or if it interrupts related sentence parts, it is misplaced and you need to reposition it.

Exercise 7 Correcting Dangling and Misplaced Modifiers

Circle the dangling (D) or misplaced (M) modifier in each of the following sentences. Identify the type of modifier by writing D or M in the blank to the left. Rewrite each sentence in the space provided.

_____ 1. Driving through the Brazilian rain forest, leaf-cutter ants were spotted going about their work.

  _____

  _____

_____ 2. This tribe of ants is one of the few creatures on this planet that grows food.

  _____

  _____

_____ 3. Leafcutter ants learned to cleverly farm over 50 million years ago.

  _____

  _____

_____ 4. Climbing trees, the leaves are cut down and bitten into the shape of half-moons.

  _____

  _____

_____ 5. Then each ant hoists a leaf and carries it back down the tree toward the nest, weighing ten times more than it does.

  _____

  _____

_____ 6. Marching home with their leaves, a parade of fluttering green flags is what the ants resemble.

  _____

  _____

———————— 7. Carried into the subterranean tunnels of the nest, the leafcutters deposit their cargo.

————————————————————

————————————————————

———————— 8. Taking over, the leaves are cleaned, clipped, and spread with secretions from tiny gardener ants' bodies.

————————————————————

————————————————————

———————— 9. Lined up in neat rows, the ants place fungus on the hunks of leaves.

————————————————————

————————————————————

———————— 10. Cultivated for food, the ants use the leaves as fertilizer for their fungus garden.

————————————————————

————————————————————

Exercise 8 Writing Sentences with Correct Modifiers

Circle the dangling (D) or misplaced (M) modifier in each of the following sentences. Identify the type of modifier by writing D or M in the blank to the left. Rewrite each sentence in the space provided.

———————— 1. Changing the oil regularly, a car runs better and lasts longer.

————————————————————

————————————————————

———————— 2. The crusty old sailor went to the fortuneteller with bad luck.

————————————————————

————————————————————

_____   3. The bartender decided to make an appointment
                     to see a psychologist with a drinking problem.

                     _____

                     _____

_____   4. Reaching speeds of 180 miles per hour, the
                     fans were thrilled by the race cars.

                     _____

                     _____

_____   5. I decided to sell my parrot with reluctance.

                     _____

                     _____

_____   6. Breathing deeply the intoxicating scent of new
                     shoes, she felt her adrenaline begin to uncon-
                     trollably flow.

                     _____

                     _____

_____   7. Carlos was determined to quickly amass his
                     fortune at the blackjack table and retire early.

                     _____

                     _____

_____   8. Swimming in a butter and garlic sauce, the
                     diners relished every bite of the shrimp.

                     _____

                     _____

_____   9. He wanted to badly propose to her and make
                     her his bride.

                     _____

                     _____

_____ 10. I decided to foolishly purchase the solar-
                     powered electric blanket.

                     _____

                     _____

✳ Chapter Review

Exercise 9 Writing Sentences with Adjectives and Adverbs

Write a sentence using each of the following words.

1. good, better, best _____

_____

_____

_____

_____

_____

_____

2. good, well _____

_____

_____

_____

_____

_____

_____

3. more, most _____

_____

_____

_____

_____

_____

_____

4. bad, badly _____

_____

_____

_____

_____

_____

_____

5. real, really _____

_____

_____

_____

_____

_____

_____

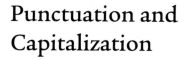 **10**

Punctuation and Capitalization

Understanding punctuation will help you write better. If you aren't sure how to punctuate a compound or a compound-complex sentence, then you probably will not write one. If you don't know how to show that some of your words come from other sources, you may mislead your reader. And if you misuse punctuation, you will force your readers to struggle to get your message. So take the time to review and master the mechanics. Your efforts will be rewarded.

✳ End Punctuation

Periods

1. Place a period after a statement.

    The weather is beautiful today.

2. Place a period after common abbreviations.

Dr.	Mr.	Mrs.	Dec.	a.m.
Exceptions:	FBI	UN	NAACP	FHA	NATO

3. Use an ellipsis—three periods within a sentence and four periods at the end of a sentence—to indicate that words have been omitted from quoted material.

    He stopped walking and the buildings . . . rose up out of the misty courtroom. . . . (James Thurber, "The Secret Life of Walter Mitty")

Question Marks

1. Place a question mark at the end of a direct question.

   Will you go to the country tomorrow?

2. Use a single question mark in sentence constructions that contain a double question—that is, a quoted question following a question.

   Mr. Martin said, "Did he say, 'Are you going?'"

3. Do *not* use a question mark after an indirect (reported) question.

   She asked me what caused the slide.

Exclamation Points

1. Place an exclamation point after a word or a group of words that expresses strong feeling.

   Oh!   What a night!   Help!   Gadzooks!

2. Do not overwork the exclamation point. Do not use double exclamation points. Use the period or comma for mild exclamatory words, phrases, or sentences.

   Oh, we can leave now.

✳ Commas

Commas to Separate

1. Use a comma to separate main clauses joined by one of the coordinating conjunctions—*for, and, nor, but, or, yet, so.* The comma may be omitted if the clauses are brief and parallel.

   We traveled many miles to see the game, *but* it was canceled.

   Mary left and I remained. (brief and parallel clauses)

2. Use a comma after introductory dependent clauses and long introductory phrases (generally, four or more words is considered long).

   Before the arrival of the shipment, the boss had written a letter protesting the delay. (two prepositional phrases)

   If you don't hear from me, assume that I am lost. (introductory clause, an adverbial modifier)

   In winter we skate on the river. (short modifier, no comma)

3. Use a comma to separate words, phrases, and clauses in a series.

> *Red, white,* and *blue* were her favorite colors. (words)
>
> He ran *down the street, across the park,* and *into the arms* of his father. (phrases)
>
> *When John was asleep, when Mary was at work,* and *when Bob was studying,* Mother had time to relax. (clauses)

4. Do *not* use a comma when coordinating conjunctions connect all the elements in a series.

> He bought apples *and* pears *and* grapes.

5. Use a comma to separate coordinate adjectives not joined by *and* that modify the same noun.

> I need a *sturdy, reliable* truck.

6. Use a comma to separate adjectives that are coordinate. Try this technique to determine whether the adjectives are coordinate: Put *and* between the adjectives. If it fits naturally, the adjectives are coordinate and require a comma; if it does not, they are not coordinate, and you do not need a comma.

> She is a kind, beautiful person. (kind *and* beautiful—natural, hence the comma)
>
> I built a red brick wall. (red *and* brick wall—not natural, no comma)

7. Use a comma to separate sentence elements that might be misread.

> Inside the dog scratched his fleas.
>
> *Inside,* the dog scratched his fleas.

Without benefit of the comma, the reader might initially misunderstand the relationship among the first three words.

Commas to Set Off

1. Use commas to set off (enclose) adjectives in pairs that follow a noun.

> The scouts, *tired and hungry,* marched back to camp.

2. Use commas to set off nonessential (unnecessary for meaning of the sentence) words, phrases, and clauses.

My brother, *a student at Ohio University,* is visiting me. (If you drop the phrase, the basic meaning of the sentence remains intact.)

Marla, *who studied hard,* will pass. (The clause is not essential to the basic meaning of the sentence.)

All students *who studied hard* will pass. (Here the clause *is* essential. If you remove it, you would have *All students will pass,* which is not necessarily true.)

I shall not stop searching *until I find the treasure.* (A dependent clause at the end of a sentence is usually not set off with a comma. However, a clause beginning with the word *though, although,* or *whereas* will be set off regardless of where it is located.)

I felt unsatisfied, *though we had won the game.* (The clause begins with *though.*)

3. Use commas to set off parenthetical elements such as mild interjections (*oh, well, yes, no,* and others), most conjunctive adverbs (*however, otherwise, therefore, similarly, hence, on the other hand,* and *consequently,* but not *then, thus, soon, now,* and *also*), quotation indicators, and special abbreviations (*etc., i.e., e.g.,* and others).

Oh, what a silly question! (mild interjection)

It is necessary, *of course,* to leave now. (sentence modifier)

We left early; *however,* we missed the train anyway. (conjunctive adverb)

"When I was in school," *he said,* "I read widely." (quotation indicators)

Books, papers, pens, *etc.,* were scattered on the floor. (The abbreviation *etc.,* however, should be used sparingly.)

4. Use commas to set off nouns used as direct address.

Play it again, *Sam.*

Please tell us the answer, *Jane,* so we can discuss it.

5. Use commas to separate the numbers in a date.

June *4, 1965,* is a day I will remember.

6. Do not use commas if the day of the month is not specified or if the day is given before the month.

June was my favorite time.

One day I will never forget is 4 June 1965.

7. Use commas to separate the city from the state. No comma is used between the state and the ZIP code.

> Walnut, CA 91789

8. Use a comma following the salutation of a friendly letter and the complimentary closing in any letter.

> Dear John,
> Sincerely,

9. Use a comma in numbers to set off groups of three digits. However, omit the comma in dates, serial numbers, page numbers, years, and street numbers.

> The total assets were $2,000,000.
> I look forward to the year 2000.

Exercise 1 Using Commas

Insert commas where needed.

1. In *Frankenstein* the original classic horror thriller written by Mary Shelley and published on October 3 1818 Victor Frankenstein was a gifted dedicated student.

2. While he studied science at the university he came upon the secret of how to create life.

3. Being more interested in simple practical matters than in theory he set out to construct a living breathing creature.

4. Victor who was very much concerned about process first needed to gather the materials necessary for his experiment.

5. He went all around town picking up body parts and he stored them in his laboratory.

6. The dissecting room at a local hospital provided him with the most basic articles and he was very grateful.

7. Local butcher shops had plenty of items perhaps including some spare ribs.

8. Finally he was ready to begin construction of a strange humanlike creature.

9. He made a creature that was eight feet tall four feet wide and very strong.

10. The face of the creature which could be described only as hideous was not easy to look upon.

11. One night while Victor was sleeping lightly the monster lonely and troubled came to his bedroom.

12. Victor screamed loudly and the monster ran away in disappointment.

13. Victor developed brain fever which was a result of the encounter.

14. When Victor recovered from his illness he discovered that one of his brothers had been murdered by an unknown person.

15. In despair and befuddlement Victor went to a remote wilderness to sort out his problems.

16. One day when he was out walking Victor saw a strange lumbering creature running into the mountains.

17. Victor chased the creature but he was unable to catch it.

18. Soon after he sat down to rest and the creature appeared before him.

19. It was Victor Frankenstein's monster who had come to talk to him.

20. With a great deal of self-pity the monster explained that he was very sad because people were unkind to him.

Exercise 2 Using Commas

Insert commas where needed.

1. Frankenstein's monster distraught and desperate told a story of acute loneliness.

2. After leaving Victor Frankenstein's house he had gone to live in the country.

3. He had tried diligently to help the simple gentle people by bringing them firewood.

4. They took the firewood; however they were at first frightened and then angry.

5. The monster very upset and dejected had gone back to the city.

6. There he killed Victor's innocent unsuspecting brother and he then cleverly tried to place the blame on someone else.

7. Listening to the monster in horror Victor Frankenstein realized what he had done in this act of creation.

8. The monster started making demands and it was clear that he would force Victor to carry them out.

9. He said that if Victor did not make a suitable female companion for him he would begin killing human beings at random.

10. Victor went away gathered up some more parts and started building a bride for the monster.

11. The monster waited in eager anticipation but he was to be sorely disappointed.

12. Victor became disgusted with his project and he destroyed all the tissue just before it came to life.

13. Needless to say the monster was deeply distressed by this unexpected shocking development.

14. Before the monster ran away he swore to get revenge on Victor's wedding night.

15. When Victor got married he armed himself fully for he expected a visit from the enraged vengeful monster.

16. On the night of the wedding the monster slipped into the bridal chambers and strangled the horrified unlucky bride.

17. Victor himself vowed to avenge the murder by killing the monster but the monster was nowhere to be found.

18. Victor finally died in a cabin in the desolate frozen lands of the North and much later his body was found by a friend.

19. The monster dropped by for one last visit for he wanted to complain about his unhappy life.

20. He said that Victor had created a man without a friend love or even a soul and therefore Victor was more wicked than anyone.

✳ Semicolons

The semicolon indicates a stronger division than the comma. It is used principally to separate independent clauses within a sentence.

1. Use a semicolon to separate independent clauses not joined by a coordinating conjunction.

    You must buy that car today; tomorrow will be too late.

2. Use a semicolon between two independent clauses joined by a conjunctive adverb such as one of the HOTSHOT CAT words (*however, otherwise, therefore, similarly, hence, on the other hand, then, consequently, accordingly, thus*).

    It was very late; therefore, I remained at the hotel.

3. Use a semicolon to separate main clauses joined by a coordinating conjunction if one or both of these clauses contain distracting commas.

Byron, the famous English poet, was buried in Greece; and Shelley, who was his friend and fellow poet, was buried in Italy.

4. Use a semicolon in a series between items that themselves contain commas.

He has lived in Covina, California; Reno, Nevada; Tribbey, Oklahoma; and Bangor, Maine.

Exercise 3 Using Semicolons and Commas

Insert semicolons and commas where needed.

1. Once upon a time, there was a young woman named Cyberella she lived in Oklahoma with an evil stepmother and an obnoxious stepsister.

2. One night at eleven her wretched stepfamily was snoring raucously and Cyberella was busily dusting the family computer which someone had left running.

3. It was then that Cyberella inadvertently hit the Instant Internet button therefore the screen lit up.

4. She had never been permitted to use the Internet but she had enviously watched her evil stepfamily at the keyboard.

5. Cyberella created the screen name Cool4aday and logged on for fun and education naturally she started with the index of chat rooms.

6. She was delighted with her unexpected opportunity however she realized that the computer was programmed to go out of commission at midnight.

7. Now she was a free-spirited cyberspace explorer surfing the World Wide Web at midnight she would turn back into a servant ripping out cobwebs and capturing dust bunnies.

8. Cyberella spotted a chat room called "Talk to the Prince" feeling like a princess she joined in the conversation.

9. To her amazement she discovered that she was chatting with a real prince Prince Igor of Transylvania in fact he seemed to like her.

10. Prince Igor boldly invited Cyberella to accompany him to a private chat room breathlessly she said yes and followed him with demure keystrokes.

11. They chatted shyly and then passionately for almost an hour and soon the prince became royally enamored by the way she processed thought noticing that she wrote skillfully, using her spell checker and grammar checker in a most delicate way.

12. Cyberella wanted to tell Prince Igor explicitly what was in her heart therefore she often used the computer thesaurus feature, impressing him further with her highly eloquent diction.

13. Prince Igor was about to ask the royal marriage question then Cyberella heard the clock strike her computer went dark and she believed she would never again chat with her sweet prince.

14. Prince Igor was devastated and vowed to find this lovely correspondent he therefore directed his army to undertake a royal search that would properly but legally identify Cool4aday and expose all impostors.

15. The soldiers would test the computer-assisted writing skills of everyone in the world if necessary moreover they would even provide laptops for any computerless woman who looked as if she could possibly be the mystery writer.

16. Cyberella had informed Prince Igor that she was from the American Southwest a fact that enabled him to focus his search.

17. Following electronic clues, the soldiers visited Amarillo Texas Tucumcari New Mexico Tulsa Oklahoma and Window Rock Arizona.

18. At last a soldier came to Cyberella's house and was greeted by the obnoxious stepsister, who claimed that she was Cool4aday and began to chat on line with Prince Igor however the stepsister forgot to use her spell checker and the prince flamed a rejection.

19. Then the soldier handed Cyberella a laptop computer and instructions of course both the wicked stepmother and the obnoxious stepsister scoffed.

20. Nevertheless, Cyberella was verified as Cool4aday and the prince was wildly elated therefore he declared an international holiday slapped his leg with glee and offered to grant her fondest wish.

21. "Does that mean I get this laptop for myself?" Cyberella asked and Prince Igor, a bit humbled by her reponse said "No that means you get me for yourself."

22. "Oh, that's very very nice but may I also have this laptop?" Cyberella asked striking a hard bargain as she fondly hugged the computer.

23. "Yes" Prince Igor said. "I'll even toss in a laser printer and I'll add a few pounds of copy paper and a stack of dungeon-and-dragon software customized in one of my own castles."

24. They got married and lived happily ever after for a while then the wicked stepfamily tried to move into the palace but they were arrested and were no longer allowed to use the Internet in Transylvania or Oklahoma until they had passed a writing test which they never did.

✳ Quotation Marks

Quotation marks are used principally to set off direct quotations. A direct quotation consists of material taken from the written work or the direct speech of others; it is set off by double quotation marks. Single quotation marks are used to set off a quotation within a quotation.

DOUBLE QUOTATION MARKS   He said, "I don't remember."

SINGLE QUOTATION MARKS   He said, "I don't remember if she said, 'Wait for me.'"

1. Use double quotation marks to set off direct quotations.

   John said, "Give me the book."

   As Edward McNeil writes of the Greek achievement: "To an extent never before realized, mind was supreme over faith."

2. Use double quotation marks to set off titles of shorter pieces of writing such as magazine articles, essays, short stories, short poems, one-act plays, chapters in books, songs, and separate pieces of writing published as part of a larger work.

   The book *Literature: Structure, Sound, and Sense* contains a deeply moving poem titled "On Wenlock Edge."

   Have you read "The Use of Force," a short story by William Carlos Williams?

   My favorite Elvis song is "Don't Be Cruel."

3. Use double quotation marks to set off slang, technical terms, and special words.

   There are many aristocrats, but Elvis is the only true "King." (special word)

   The "platoon system" changed the game of football. (technical term)

4. Use double quotation marks in writing dialogue (conversation). Write each speech unit as a separate paragraph and set it off with double quotation marks.

   "Will you go with me?" he asked.

   "Yes," she replied. "Are you ready now?"

5. Use single quotation marks to set off a quotation within a quotation.

Professor Baxter said, "You should remember Shakespeare's words 'All the world's a stage.'"

6. Do *not* use quotation marks for indirect quotations.

> WRONG   He said that "he would bring the supplies."
>
> RIGHT   He said that he would bring the supplies.

7. Do *not* use quotation marks for the title on your own written work. If you refer to that title in another piece of writing, however, you need the quotation marks.

✳ Punctuation with Quotation Marks

1. A period or comma is always placed *inside* the quotation marks.

> Our assignment for Monday was to read Poe's poem "The Raven."
>
> "I will read you the story," he said. "It's a good one."

2. A semicolon or colon is always placed *outside* the quotation marks.

> He read Robert Frost's poem "Design"; then he gave the examination.

3. A question mark, exclamation point, or dash is placed *outside* the quotation marks when it applies to the entire sentence and *inside* the quotation marks when it applies to the material in quotation marks.

> He asked, "Am I responsible for everything?" (quoted question within a statement)
>
> Did you hear him say, "I have the answer"? (statement within a question)
>
> Did she say, "Are you ready?" (question within a question)
>
> She shouted, "Impossible!" (exclamation)
>
> "I hope—that is, I—" he began. (dash)

✳ Italics

Italic print (slanting type) is used to call special attention to certain words or groups of words. In handwriting, such words are underlined.

1. Italicize (underline) foreign words and phrases that are still listed in the dictionary as foreign.

> *nouveau riche*   *Weltschmerz*

2. Italicize (underline) titles of books (except the Bible), long poems, plays, magazines, motion pictures, musical compositions, newspapers, works of art, names of aircraft, ships, and letters, figures, and words.

> I think Hemingway's best novel is *A Farewell to Arms.*
>
> His source material was taken from *Time, Newsweek,* and the Los Angeles *Times.* (Sometimes the name of the city in titles of newspapers is italicized—for example, the *New York Times.*)
>
> The *Mona Lisa* is my favorite painting.

3. Italicize (underline) the names of ships, airplanes, spacecraft, and trains.

> Ships: *Queen Mary   Lurline   Stockholm*
> Spacecraft: *Challenger   Voyager 2*

4. Italicize (underline) to distinguish letters, figures, and words when they refer to themselves rather than to the ideas or things they usually represent.

> Do not leave the *o* out of *sophomore.*
> Your *3*'s look like *5*'s.

Exercise 4 Using Quotation Marks and Italics

Insert quotation marks and italics (underlining) as needed.

1. Professor Jones said, Now we will read from The Complete Works of Edgar Allan Poe.

2. The enthusiastic students shouted, We like Poe! We like Poe!

3. The professor lectured for fifty-seven minutes before he finally said, In conclusion, Poe was an unappreciated writer during his lifetime.

4. The next speaker said, I believe that Poe said, A short story should be short enough so that a person can read it in one sitting.

5. Then, while students squirmed, he read The Fall of the House of Usher in sixty-eight minutes.

6. Now we will do some reading in unison, said Professor Jones.

7. The students were not pleased that they would be reading only the word *Nevermore* from the poem The Raven.

8. The professor reached into his bag of props, took out a dark, feathered object, and said, I have brought a stuffed raven.

9. That's not a raven. That's a crow, said a student who was majoring in ornithology.

10. The professor waggled his finger playfully at his audience and said, I believe Coleridge once observed, Art sometimes requires the willing suspension of disbelief.

✳ Dashes

The dash is used when a stronger break than the comma is needed. The dash is typed as two hyphens with no space before or after them (--).

1. Use a dash to indicate a sudden change in sentence construction or an abrupt break in thought.

> Here is the true reason—but maybe you don't care.

2. Use a dash after an introductory list. The words *these, those, all,* and occasionally *such* introduce the summarizing statement.

> English, French, history—these are the subjects I like.
> Dodgers, Giants, Yankees—such names bring back memories of exciting World Series games.

3. Use a dash to set off material that interrupts the flow of an idea, sets off material for emphasis, or restates an idea as an appositive.

> You are—I am certain—not serious. (interrupting)
>
> Our next question is—how much money did we raise? (emphasis)
>
> Dione plays the kazoo—an instrument with a buzz. (restatement)

4. Use a dash to indicate an unfinished statement, an omitted word, or an interruption. Such interruptions usually occur in dialogue.

> Susan said, "Shall we—" (no period)
>
> "I only wanted—" Jason remarked. (no comma)

5. Do *not* use a dash in places in which other marks of punctuation would be more appropriate.

> WRONG   Lupe found the store—and she shopped.
>
> RIGHT   Lupe found the store, and she shopped.
>
> WRONG   I think it is too early to go—
>
> RIGHT   I think it is too early to go.

✳ Colons

The colon is a formal mark of punctuation used chiefly to introduce something that is to follow, such as a list, a quotation, or an explanation.

1. Use a colon after a main clause to introduce a formal list, an emphatic or long restatement (appositive), an explanation, an emphatic statement, or a summary.

> These cars are my favorites: Cadillac, Chevrolet, Buick, Oldsmobile, and Pontiac. (list)
>
> He worked toward one objective: a degree. (restatement or appositive)
>
> Let me emphasize one point: I do not accept late papers. (emphatic statement)

2. Use a colon to introduce a formal quotation or a formal question.

> Shakespeare's Polonius said: "Neither a borrower nor a lender be." (formal quotation)
>
> The question is this: Shall we surrender? (formal question)

3. Use a colon in the following conventional ways: to separate a title and subtitle, a chapter and verse in the Bible, and hours and minutes; and after the salutation in a formal business letter.

TITLE AND SUBTITLE	*KOREA: A COUNTRY DIVIDED*
CHAPTER AND VERSE	Genesis 4:12
HOUR AND MINUTES	8:25 p.m.
SALUTATION	Dear Ms. Johnson:

✳ Parentheses

1. Parentheses are used to set off material that is not part of the main sentence but is too relevant to omit altogether. In this category are numbers that designate items in a series, amplifying references, explanations, directions, and qualifications.

> He offered two reasons for his losing: (1) he was tired; (2) he was out of condition. (numbers)
>
> Review the chapters on the Civil War (6, 7, and 8) for the next class meeting. (references)
>
> Her husband (she had been married about a year) died last week. (explanation)

2. Use a comma, semicolon, and colon after the parentheses when the sentence punctuation requires their use.

> Although I have not lived here long (I arrived in 1996), this place feels like my only true home.

Use a period, question mark, and exclamation point in appropriate positions, depending on whether they go with the material within the parentheses or with the entire sentence.

> The greatest English poet of the seventeenth century was John Milton (1608–1674).
>
> The greatest English poet of the seventeenth century was John Milton. (Some might not agree; I myself favor Andrew Marvell.)

✳ Brackets

Brackets are used within a quotation to set off editorial additions or corrections made by the person who is quoting.

> Churchill said: "It [the Yalta agreement] contained many mistakes."

✳ Apostrophes

The apostrophe is used with nouns and indefinite pronouns to show possession; to show the omission of letters and figures in contractions; and to form the plurals of letters, figures, and words referred to as words.

1. A possessive shows that something is owned by someone. Use an apostrophe and -*s* to form the possessive of a noun, singular or plural, that does not end in -*s*.

   man's coat   women's suits

2. Use an apostrophe alone to form the possessive of a plural noun ending in -*s*.

   girls' clothes   the Browns' house

3. Use an apostrophe and -*s* or the apostrophe alone to form the possessive of singular nouns ending in -*s*. Use the apostrophe and -*s* only when you would pronounce the *s*.

   James' hat or (if you would pronounce the *s*) James's hat

4. Use an apostrophe and -*s* to form the possessive of certain indefinite pronouns.

   everybody's idea   one's meat   another's poison

5. Use an apostrophe to indicate that letters or figures have been omitted.

   o'clock (short for *of the clock*)   in the '80s (short for *1980s*)

6. Use an apostrophe to indicate the plural of letters, figures, and words used as words.

   Dot your *i*'s.   five *8*'s   *and*'s

7. Use an apostrophe with pronouns only when you are making a contraction. A contraction is a combination of two words. The

apostrophe in a contraction indicates where a letter has been omitted.

> it is = it's
> she has = she's
> you are = you're

If no letters have been left out, don't use an apostrophe.

> WRONG   The dog bit it's tail. (not a contraction)
> RIGHT   The dog bit its tail.
> WRONG   Whose the leader now?
> RIGHT   Who's the leader now? (a contraction of *who is*)
> WRONG   Its a big problem.
> RIGHT   It's a big problem. (a contraction of *it is*)

✳ Hyphens

The hyphen brings two or more words together into a single compound word. Correct hyphenation, therefore, is essentially a spelling problem rather than one of punctuation. Because the hyphen is not used with any degree of consistency, consult your dictionary for current usage. Study the following as a beginning guide.

1. Use a hyphen to separate the parts of many compound words.

> brother-in-law   go-between

2. Use a hyphen between prefixes and suffixes and proper names.

> all-American   mid-Atlantic

3. Use a hyphen to join two or more words used as a single adjective modifier before a noun.

> bluish-gray eyes   first-class service

4. Use a hyphen with spelled-out compound numbers up to ninety-nine, and with fractions.

> twenty-six   two-thirds

Note: Dates, street addresses, numbers requiring more than two words, chapter and page numbers, time followed directly by *a.m.* or *p.m.*, and figures after a dollar sign or before measurement abbreviations are usually written as figures, not words.

✳ Capitalization

In English, there are many conventions concerning the use of capital letters. Here are some of them.

1. Capitalize the first word of a sentence.
2. Capitalize proper nouns and adjectives derived from proper nouns.

Names of persons
Edward Jones

Adjectives derived from proper nouns
a Shakespearean sonnet   a Miltonic sonnet

Countries, nationalities, races, languages
Germany   English   Spanish   Chinese

States, regions, localities, other geographical divisions
California   the Far East   the South

Oceans, lakes, mountains, deserts, streets, parks
Lake Superior   Fifth Avenue   Sahara Desert

Educational institutions, schools, courses
Santa Ana College   Spanish 3   Joe Hill School
Rowland High School

Organizations and their members
Boston Red Sox   Boy Scouts   Audubon Society

Corporations, governmental agencies or departments, trade names
U.S. Steel Corporation   Treasury Department
White Memorial Library   Coke

Calendar references such as holidays, days of the week, months
Easter   Tuesday   January

Historic eras, periods, documents, laws
Declaration of Independence   Geneva Convention
First Crusade   Romantic Age

3. Capitalize words denoting family relationships when they are used before a name or substituted for a name.

He walked with his nephew and Aunt Grace.
but
He walked with his nephew and his aunt.

Grandmother and Mother are away on vacation.
but
My grandmother and my mother are away on vacation.

4. Capitalize abbreviations after names.

> Henry White Jr.
> Juan Gomez, M.D.

5. Capitalize titles of themes, books, plays, movies, poems, magazines, newspapers, musical compositions, songs, and works of art. Do not capitalize short conjunctions and prepositions unless they come at the beginning or the end of the title.

> *Desire Under the Elms*   *Terminator*
> *Last of the Mohicans*   *Of Mice and Men*
> "Blueberry Hill"

6. Capitalize any title preceding a name or used as a substitute for a name. Do not capitalize a title following a name.

> Judge Wong   Alfred Wong, a judge
> General Clark   Raymond Clark, a general
> Professor Fuentes   Harry Jones, the former president

Exercise 5 Using Capital Letters and All Punctuation Marks

Correct capitalization and insert punctuation marks as needed.

will rogers 1879–1935 was a famous movie star newspaper writer and

lecturer. A part cherokee indian he was born in what was then indian

territory before oklahoma became a state. He is especially known for

his humor and his social and political criticism. He said my ancestors

may not have come over on the *mayflower,* but they met em at the

boat. He said that when many oklahomans moved to california in the

early1930s the average IQ increased in both states. In his early years,

he was a first class performer in rodeos circuses and variety shows.

When he performed in variety shows he often twirled a rope. He usually began his presentations by saying, all I know is what I read in the papers. Continuing to be close to his oklahoma roots he appeared in fifty-one silent movies and twenty-one talking movies. At the age of fifty-six he was killed in an airplane crash near Point Barrow Alaska. He was so popular and influential that his statue now stands in washington d.c. On another statue of him in Claremore Oklahoma is inscribed one of his most famous sayings I never met a man I didn't like.

Exercise 6   Using Capital Letters and All Punctuation Marks

Correct capitalization and insert punctuation marks as needed.

1. everyone defines the term success differently how do you define it

2. according to american author and editor christopher morley the only success is being able to spend your life the way you want to spend it

3. margaret thatcher former leader of great britain said that success is being good at what youre doing but also having a sense of purpose

4. author vernon howard had this to say on the subject "you have succeeded in life when all you really want is only what you really need

5. albert einstein however believed that if A equals success in life then A = x + y + z

6. x is work y is play and z is keeping your mouth shut

7. one of the most well known quotes about success comes from philosopher ralph waldo emerson who wrote that to have succeeded is "to leave the world a bit better" and "to know that even one life has breathed easier because you have lived

✳ Chapter Review

Exercise 7 Writing Sentences with Correct Punctuation

Demonstrate your ability to use punctuation by writing sentences that contain these marks. Use the topics in parentheses.

Comma (travel)

1. To separate independent clauses in a compound sentence using coordinating conjunctions (FANBOYS) _____

_____

_____

2. For long introductory modifiers _____

_____

_____

3. To separate words in a series _____

_____

_____

Semicolon (a family member)

4. To connect two related independent clauses without a coordinating conjunction _____

_____

_____

Quotation Marks (Use this textbook as your source for quotations.)

5. To set off a quotation (words taken from the written work or the speech of others) _____

_____

_____

Italics, shown by underlining (school)

6. To refer to a word or letter by its name _____

_____

_____

7. For the title of a book _____

_____

_____

Colon (a job)

8. To introduce a list _____

_____

_____

Apostrophe (friendship)

9. To show a singular or plural possessive _____

_____

_____

10. To write a contraction _____

_____

_____

Hyphen (shopping)

11. To use in numbers _____

_____

_____

12. To indicate two-word modifiers _____

_____

_____

Spelling and Commonly Confused Words

✳ Spelling Tips

The following tips will help you become a better speller:

- **Do not omit letters.**

  Many errors occur because certain letters are omitted when the word is pronounced or spelled. Observe the omissions in the following words. Then concentrate on learning the correct spellings.

Incorrect	Correct	Incorrect	Correct
agravate	aggravate	ajourned	adjourned
aproved	approved	aquaintance	acquaintance
artic	arctic	comodity	commodity
efficent	efficient	envirnment	environment
familar	familiar	irigation	irrigation
libary	library	paralell	parallel
parlament	parliament	paticulaly	particularly
readly	readily	sophmore	sophomore
stricly	strictly	unconsious	unconscious

- **Do not add letters.**

Incorrect	Correct	Incorrect	Correct
athelete	athlete	comming	coming
drownded	drowned	folkes	folks
occassionally	occasionally	ommission	omission
pasttime	pastime	priviledge	privilege
similiar	similar	tradgedy	tragedy

- **Do not substitute incorrect letters for correct letters.**

Incorrect	Correct	Incorrect	Correct
benefisial	beneficial	bullitins	bulletins
sensus	census	discription	description
desease	disease	dissention	dissension
itims	items	offence	offense
peculier	peculiar	resitation	recitation
screach	screech	substansial	substantial
surprize	surprise	technacal	technical

- **Do not transpose letters.**

Incorrect	Correct	Incorrect	Correct
alunmi	alumni	childern	children
dupilcate	duplicate	irrevelant	irrelevant
kindel	kindle	prehaps	perhaps
perfer	prefer	perscription	prescription
principels	principles	yeild	yield

Note: Whenever you notice other words that fall into any one of these categories, add them to the list.

- **Apply the spelling rules for spelling *ei* and *ie* words correctly.**

Remember the poem?

Use *i* before *e*
Except after *c*
Or when sounded as *a*
As in *neighbor* and *weigh.*

i* before *e

achieve	belief	believe	brief
chief	field	grief	hygiene
niece	piece	pierce	relief
relieve	shield	siege	variety

*Except after **c***

ceiling	conceit	conceive	deceit
deceive	perceive	receipt	receive

Exceptions: either, financier, height, leisure, neither, seize, species, weird.

*When sounded as **a***

deign	eight	feign	feint
freight	heinous	heir	neigh
neighbor	rein	reign	skein
sleigh	veil	vein	weigh

- **Apply the rules for dropping the final *e* or retaining the final *e* when a suffix is added.**

Words ending in a silent *e* usually drop the *e* before a suffix beginning with a vowel; for example, *accuse* + *-ing* = *accusing*. Some common suffixes beginning with a vowel are the following: *-able, -al, -age, -ary, -ation, -ence, -ing, -ion, -ous, -ure*.

admire + *-able* = admirable	arrive + *-al* = arrival
come + *-ing* = coming	explore + *-ation* = exploration
fame + *-ous* = famous	imagine + *-ary* = imaginary
locate + *-ion* = location	please + *-ure* = pleasure
plume + *-age* = plumage	precede + *-ence* = precedence

Exceptions: dye + *-ing* = *dyeing* (to distinguish it from *dying*), *acreage, mileage.*

Words ending in a silent *e* usually retain the *e* before a suffix beginning with a consonant; for example: *arrange* + *-ment* = *arrangement*. Some common suffixes beginning with a consonant are the following: *-craft, -ful, -less, -ly, -mate, -ment, -ness, -ty*.

entire + *-ty* = entirety	hate + *-ful* = hateful
hope + *-less* = hopeless	like + *-ness* = likeness
manage + *-ment* = management	safe + *-ly* = safely
stale + *-mate* = stalemate	state + *-craft* = statecraft

Exceptions: Some words taking the *-ful* or *-ly* suffixes drop the final *e:*

awe + *-ful* = awful	due + *-ly* = duly
true + *-ly* = truly	whole + *-ly* = wholly

Some words taking the suffix *-ment* drop the final *e;* for example:

acknowledgment	argument	judgment

Words ending in silent *e* after *c* or *g* retain the *e* when the suffix begins with the vowel *a* or *o*. The final *e* is retained to keep the *c* or *g* soft before the suffixes.

advantageous	courageous
noticeable	peaceable

- **Apply the rules for doubling a final consonant before a suffix beginning with a vowel.**

Words of one syllable

blot	blotted	brag	bragging	cut	cutting
drag	dragged	drop	dropped	get	getting
hop	hopper	hot	hottest	man	mannish
plan	planned	rob	robbed	run	running
sit	sitting	stop	stopped	swim	swimming

Words accented on the last syllable

acquit	acquitted	admit	admittance
allot	allotted	begin	beginning
commit	committee	concur	concurring
confer	conferring	defer	deferring
equip	equipped	occur	occurrence
omit	omitting	prefer	preferred
refer	referred	submit	submitted
transfer	transferred		

Words that are not accented on the last syllable, or words that do not end in a single consonant preceded by a vowel, do not double the final consonant (whether or not the suffix begins with a vowel).

✳ Frequently Misspelled Words

a lot	belief	development	exaggerate
absence	benefit	difference	excellent
across	buried	disastrous	exercise
actually	business	discipline	existence
all right	certain	discussed	experience
among	college	disease	explanation
analyze	coming	divide	extremely
appearance	committee	dying	familiar
appreciate	competition	eighth	February
argument	complete	eligible	finally
athlete	consider	eliminate	foreign
athletics	criticism	embarrassed	government
awkward	definitely	environment	grammar
becoming	dependent	especially	grateful
beginning	develop	etc.	guarantee

guard	nuclear	religious	thoroughly
guidance	occasionally	repetition	though
height	opinion	rhythm	tragedy
hoping	opportunity	ridiculous	tried
humorous	parallel	sacrifice	tries
immediately	particular	safety	truly
independent	persuade	scene	unfortunately
intelligence	physically	schedule	unnecessary
interest	planned	secretary	until
interfere	pleasant	senior	unusual
involved	possible	sense	using
knowledge	practical	separate	usually
laboratory	preferred	severely	Wednesday
leisure	prejudice	shining	writing
length	privilege	significant	written
library	probably	similar	
likely	professor	sincerely	
lying	prove	sophomore	
marriage	psychology	speech	
mathematics	pursue	straight	
meant	receipt	studying	
medicine	receive	succeed	
neither	recommend	success	
ninety	reference	suggest	
ninth	relieve	surprise	

Exercise 1 Using Correct Spelling

Underline the misspelled words and write the correct spelling above the words. Double underline the words that are incorrectly spelled but would go unchallenged by your spell checker.

Professor Pufnagel was torturing his English students once again, and he relished his familar evil roll. "Today, class, we will write without the assistence of computers. In fact, never again will we use them in this class. They are a perscription for lazyness. And they make life to easy for alot of you."

The profesor lectured the students for an hour, stresing that when he was in school, there were no computers in his enviroment. He extoled the virtues of writting with little yellow pensils, fountain pens, and solid, dependible typewriters. He went on with his ranting, listing computer games, television sets, frozen foods, plastic wrap, asperin, and Velcro as similiar and familiar negative forces that had lead society to it's truely sorry state. "You are nothing but a pityful pack of party people, and you will recieve no sympathy from me," he sputtered. Grabbing a student's laptop computer, Pufnagel reared back and, like an athalete, hurled it against the wall. In the corner of the classroom lay a pile of high-tech junk, once fine shinning machines, now just garbage—smashed in a senseless, aweful war against technology.

The students starred in embarassed amazement at there professor, who was developing a nervous twitch. His mouth began twisting and contorting as his limbs jerked with the helter-skelter motion of a tangled marionette. He clutched desparately at his throat, and smoke began to poor out of his ears and neck. Unconsious, he crashed to the floor with a clatter.

One of the students, who had just taken a CPR class, rushed forward and attempted to revive the fallen educator. As the student pounded with a catchy rap rhythm on the chest of his stricken teacher, everyone herd a loud pop and sizzle.

It was a door in Pufnagel's chest, which had poped open to reveal the complex electrical control panel of a short-circuited cyborg!

Just than a security team in white jumpsuits from student goverment entered the class, carefully deposited Pufnagel on a wheelbarrow, and roled him out to the Faculty Service Center.

A few minutes later a Professor Ramirez arrived. "Ladys and gentlemen," she said, "its time to start your search engines. Your prevous professor's mainframe is down, but I'm his substitute and mine is fine, fine, fine, fine, fine, fine, fine, fine, fine, fine. . . ."

✳ Confused Spelling/Confusing Words

The following are more words that are commonly misspelled or confused with one another. Some have similar sounds, some are often mispronounced, and some are only misunderstood.

a	An article adjective used before a word beginning with a consonant or a consonant sound, as in "I ate *a* donut."
an	An article adjective used before a word beginning with a vowel (*a, e, i, o, u*) or with a silent *h*, as in "I ate *an* artichoke."
and	A coordinating conjunction, as in "Sara *and* I like Johnny Cash."
accept	A verb meaning "to receive," as in "I *accept* your explanation."
except	A preposition meaning "to exclude," as in "I paid everyone *except* you."

advice	A noun meaning "guidance," as in "Thanks for the *advice.*"
advise	A verb meaning "to give guidance," as in "Will you please *advise* me of my rights?"
all right	An adjective meaning "correct" or "acceptable," as in "It's *all right* to cry."
alright	Not used in formal writing.
all ready	An adjective that can be used interchangeably with *ready,* as in "I am *all ready* to go to town."
already	An adverb meaning "before," which cannot be used in place of *ready,* as in "I have *already* finished."
a lot	An adverb meaning "much," as in "She liked him *a lot,*" or a noun meaning "several," as in "I had *a lot* of suggestions."
alot	Misspelling.
altogether	An adverb meaning "completely," as in "He is *altogether* happy."
all together	An adverb meaning "as one," which can be used interchangeably with *together,* as in "The group left *all together.*"
could of	Misspelling.
could have	A verb phrase, as in "I *could have* used some kindness."
choose	A present-tense verb meaning "to select," as in "Do whatever you *choose.*"
chose	The past-tense form of the verb *choose,* as in "They *chose* to take action yesterday."
effect	Usually a noun meaning "result," as in "That *effect* was unexpected."
affect	Usually a verb meaning "change," as in "Ideas *affect* me."
hear	A verb indicating the receiving of sound, as in "I *hear* thunder."
here	An adverb meaning "present location," as in "I live *here.*"

it's	A contraction of *it is,* as in "*It's* time to dance."
its	Possessive pronoun, as in "Each dog has *its* day."
know	A verb usually meaning "to comprehend" or "to recognize," as in "I *know* the answer."
no	An adjective meaning "negative," as in "I have *no* potatoes."
led	The past-tense form of the verb *lead,* as in "I *led* a wild life in my youth."
lead	A present-tense verb, as in "I *lead* a stable life now" or a noun referring to a substance, such as "I sharpened the *lead* in my pencil."
loose	An adjective meaning "without restraint," as in "He is a *loose* cannon."
lose	A present-tense verb from the pattern *lose, lost, lost,* as in "I thought I would *lose* my senses."
paid	The past-tense form of *pay,* as in "He *paid* his dues."
payed	Misspelling.
passed	The past-tense form of the verb *pass,* meaning "went by," as in "He *passed* me on the curve."
past	An adjective meaning "former," as in "That's *past* history"; or a noun, as in "the past."
patience	A noun meaning "willingness to wait," as in "Job was a man of much *patience.*"
patients	A noun meaning "people under care," as in "The doctor had fifty *patients.*"
peace	A noun meaning "a quality of calmness" or "absence of strife," as in "The guru was at *peace* with the world."
piece	A noun meaning "particle," as in "I gave him a *piece* of my mind."
quiet	An adjective meaning "silent," as in "She was a *quiet* child."

quit	A verb meaning "to cease" or "to withdraw," as in "I *quit* my job."
quite	An adverb meaning "very," as in "The clam is *quite* happy."
receive	A verb meaning "to accept," as in "I will *receive* visitors now."
recieve	Misspelling.
stationary	An adjective meaning "not moving," as in "Try to avoid running into *stationary* objects."
stationery	A noun meaning "paper material to write on," as in "I bought a box of *stationery* for Sue's birthday present."
than	A conjunction, as in "He is taller *than* I am."
then	An adverb, as in "She *then* left town."
their	An adjective, as in "They read *their* books."
there	An adverb, as in "He left it *there*," or a filler word as in "*There* is no time left."
they're	A contraction of *they are,* as in "*They're* happy."
to	A preposition, as in "I went *to* town."
too	An adverb meaning "having exceeded or gone beyond what is acceptable," as in "You are *too* late to qualify for the discount," or "also," as in "I have feelings, *too.*"
two	An adjective of number, as in "I have *two* jobs."
thorough	An adjective, as in "He did a *thorough* job."
through	A preposition, as in "She went *through* the yard."
truly	An adverb meaning "sincerely" or "completely," as in "He was *truly* happy."
truely	Misspelling.
weather	A noun meaning "condition of the atmosphere," as in "The *weather* is pleasant today."
whether	A conjunction, as in "*Whether* he would go was of no consequence."

write	A present-tense verb, as in "Watch me as I *write* this letter."
writen	Misspelling.
written	A past-participle verb, as in "I have *written* the letter."
you're	A contraction of *you are*, as in "*You're* my friend."
your	A possessive pronoun, as in "I like *your* looks."

Exercise 2 Spelling Confusing Words

Underline the correct word or words.

1. I cannot (hear, here) the answers.

2. She is taller (then, than) I.

3. They left town to find (their, they're, there) roots.

4. Sam went (through, thorough) the initiation.

5. I am only asking for a little (peace, piece) of the action.

6. Whatever you say is (alright, all right) with me.

7. I (passed, past) the test, and now I'm ready for action.

8. That smash was (to, too, two) hot to handle.

9. I did not ask for her (advise, advice).

10. I found (a lot, alot) of new ideas in that book.

11. She has (all ready, already) left.

12. I (chose, choose) my answer and hoped for the best.

13. I knew that I would (recieve, receive) fair treatment.

14. Juan was (quit, quite, quiet) happy with my decision.

15. Maria (could of, could have) completed the assignment.

16. Marlin knew they would (lose, loose) the game.

17. I've heard that (it's, its) a good movie.

18. June would not (accept, except) my answer.

19. I did not (know, no) what to do.

20. Sean (paid, payed) his bill and left town.

Exercise 3 Spelling Confusing Words

Underline the correct word or words.

1. She said that my application was (alright, all right).

2. Sheriff Dillon worked hard for (peace, piece) in the valley.

3. She was the first woman to (recieve, receive) a medal.

4. He spoke his mind; (then, than) he left.

5. The cleaners did a (through, thorough) job.

6. After the loud explosion, there was (quit, quiet, quite).

7. The nurse worked diligently with his (patience, patients).

8. They were not (altogether, all together) happy, but they (could of, could have) been.

9. The cowboys (led, lead) the cows to water.

10. For my hobby, I study (grammar, grammer).

11. Elvis (truly, truely) respected his mother.

12. Zeke asked for the (whether, weather) report.

13. I never (advise, advice) my friends about gambling.

14. You should (accept, except) responsibility for your actions.

15. Joan inherited (alot, a lot) of money.

16. We waited for the gorilla to (chose, choose) a mate.

17. Virginia thinks (its, it's) a good day for a party.

18. It was a tale of (to, too, two) cities.

19. I went (they're, their, there) to my childhood home.

20. It was the best letter Kevin had ever (writen, written, wrote).

✳ Wordy Phrases

Certain phrases clutter sentences, consuming our time in writing and our readers' time in reading. Watch for wordy phrases as you revise and edit your composition.

WORDY   *Due to the fact* that he was unemployed, he had to use public transportation.

CONCISE   *Because* he was unemployed, he had to use public transportation.

WORDY   *Deep down inside* he believed that the Red Sox would win.

CONCISE   He believed that the Red Sox would win.

Wordy	Concise
at the present time	now
basic essentials	essentials
blend together	blend
it is clear that	(delete)
due to the fact that	because
for the reason that	because
I felt inside	I felt

in most cases	usually
as a matter of fact	in fact
in the event that	if
until such time as	until
I personally feel	I feel
in this modern world	today
in order to	to
most of the people	most people
along the lines of	like
past experience	experience
at that point in time	then
in the final analysis	finally
in the near future	soon
have a need for	need
in this day and age	now

Exercise 4 Avoiding Wordy Phrasing

Circle the wordy phrases and write in concise phrases.

1. I tried to recall that moment, but my memories seemed to blend together.

2. I expect to get out of this bed and go to work in the near future.

3. As a matter of fact, when I was a child, I had an imaginary playmate.

4. I feel in my heart that bees work too hard.

5. I am not surprised by this conviction due to the fact that as a child he used to torment vegetables.

6. In this modern world most of the people do not use enough shoe polish.

7. I was crowned Mr. Clean for the reason that I always wash my hands before I wash my hands.

8. At the present time I am concentrating on not thinking about warthogs.

9. Procrastination is an idea I will consider in the near future.

10. I personally feel that Cupid just shot me with a poisoned arrow.

✳ 12

The Writing Process: Paragraphs and Essays

✳ The Paragraph and Essay Defined

A **paragraph** is a group of sentences that relate to a single idea. That idea, called the **controlling idea,** is often stated in one sentence, which is known as the topic sentence. All the other sentences in the paragraph explain or support the topic sentence.

An **essay** contains many paragraphs. It begins with an introductory paragraph that usually presents the main idea (or thesis). The main idea is then developed in several paragraphs that make up the body of the essay. An essay usually ends with a concluding paragraph that gives a feeling of finality, or closure. The concluding paragraph sometimes summarizes the main idea that was developed throughout the essay.

Thus, considered structurally, the paragraph is often an essay in miniature. That does not mean that all paragraphs can grow up to be essays or that all essays can shrink to become paragraphs. For college writing, however, a good understanding of the parallel between well-organized paragraphs and well-organized essays is useful. As you learn the properties of effective paragraphs—those with a strong topic sentence and strong support—you also learn how to organize an essay, if you just magnify the procedure.

The following diagram illustrates the parallel parts of outlines, paragraphs, and essays:

PARAGRAPH	OUTLINE	ESSAY
Topic Sentence	Topic Sentence or Thesis	Introduction, with Thesis or Purpose
Support Sentence 1	I. Support 1	Support Paragraph 1
Support Sentence 2	II. Support 2	Support Paragraph 2
Support Sentence 3	III. Support 3	Support Paragraph 3
Concluding Sentence	Conclusion	Conclusion

✳ The Writing Process

Effective and easily followed steps exist for writing a paragraph and even an essay. Writing does not mean merely putting words on a piece of paper. It is a process that often involves several stages: using prewriting techniques to explore a topic; limiting and then developing the topic, usually with an outline; writing a first draft; revising the draft as often as necessary; and editing the material. At times, writers discover that their topic sentence or their outline does not work, and they go back and alter their original concept or design.

Here is how one student, Vera Harris, moved from an idea to a topic sentence to an outline to a paragraph. Vera Harris returned to college while she still had a full-time job as a hairdresser. When her instructor asked her to write a paragraph about types of people she had encountered, she naturally considered her customers for the subject of her paragraph—what she would write about. But she also had a special interest in dogs, and she hoped she would be able, somehow, to include that interest. Although she knew her topic rather well, she worked with some prewriting techniques that allowed her to get her ideas flowing onto paper.

Prewriting

Freewriting

Vera wrote about a page without stopping, just letting her ideas tumble forward without concern for correctness. This enabled her to get her project under way and to deal immediately with the common problem of writer's block. She knew that most of the material would be unusable but also that she would probably hit upon some good ideas that would give her a sense of direction and new insights. These good ideas she would circle and perhaps even make notes about in the margins of her paper. Here is Vera's freewriting.

> I have worked in beauty shops for a long
>
> time, and I've naturally made a lot of
>
> observations about my customers. I could
>
> write about what they look like and how they
>
> **Types of**   behave and how they tip and lots of things.
> **customers**
>
> When I first started to work, I guess at

first I thought of them as pretty much the
same but then I started (to see them as types)
mainly as to how they acted and I remember
way back then I sometimes thought of how they
(reminded me of dogs.) I don't mean that in any
bad way but just that /human beings have

Both dogs and their personalities and their appearances and
customers can
be grouped   all and so do dogs.

Brainstorming

Vera then sharpened her focus by listing some words and phrases,
mainly in response to the questions *Who? What? Where? When?*
Why? and *How?* One (*How?*) became a list.

> *Who?* my customers
> *What?* the way they act
> *Where?* in the beauty salon
> *When?* for the years I have worked
> *Why?* their basic nature
> *How?* behavior sometimes like dogs—hounds, Dobermans,
>   terriers, bulldogs, cockers, poodles, mixed, retrievers, boxers

Clustering

After indicating her main subject inside a double bubble, Vera jotted
down ideas inside single bubbles radiating out from the topic hub.
With this arrangement, she could begin to see connections.

Topic Sentence

At that point, knowing her subject material and the assignment very
well, she wrote a topic sentence. A topic sentence controls the paragraph by indicating the subject (what the writer is writing about) and
the treatment (what the writer is doing with the subject) of the subject.

The customers in the beauty shop where I work
subject

remind me of types of dogs (of which I am fond).
treatment

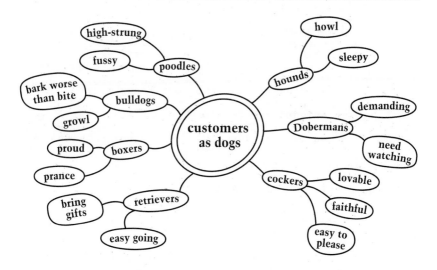

Outline

Then Vera made a basic outline. An **outline** is a pattern for showing the relationship of ideas. Vera supported her topic sentence by listing the types of dogs her customers reminded her of. Under each type, she described the characteristics typical of both the dogs and the people. The major-support and minor-support labels show you how she organized her material in correct outline form.

> TOPIC SENTENCE   The customers in the beauty shop where I work remind me of types of dogs (of which I am fond).

  I. Poodles (major support)
    A. High-strung (minor support)
    B. Need attention (minor support)
  II. Doberman pinschers (major support)
    A. Demanding (minor support)
    B. Need watching (minor support)
 III. Bulldogs (major support)
    A. Act mean (minor support)
    B. Will back down (minor support)
 IV. Cocker spaniels (major support)
    A. Lovable (minor support)
    B. Faithful (minor support)
    C. Easy to please (minor support)

If Vera had experienced problems, she would have gone back to her topic sentence or even back to prewriting techniques to make adjustments.

Writing a First Draft

Following her outline for her main and supporting points, Vera wrote her first draft. (With more development, this writing could have been a six-paragraph essay instead of a long paragraph. See the diagram on page 193.) In a first draft, writers do not try to "get everything right." They try to discuss the topic as fully as possible. Here is Vera's first draft:

Customers Are Like Canines

I have worked in a beauty salon for a long time. There, I have come across almost every kind of salon customer, each with her own unique looks and personality. I am also a dog lover and I have observed numerous dogs with care it is easier to classify these people if I compare them with canine types—but in a playful rather than a mean way. The first group is made up of poodles. Poodles are very prissy, with a constant need for attention. Their hair is usually over-styled. They think puffballs in soft colors look great. The next group and largest group is made up of cocker spanials. The Cockers are very lovable the most faithful. They like being pampered. Cockers like to see me every week and visit with others. Sometimes I can almost see their tails wagging. Then come the Doberman pinchers, this type scares me the most. Dobies are hard to please. If one hair goes the wrong way. I will see their upper lip rise up to show eyeteeth, as if they are snarling. I rarely

```
turn my back while working on this type—a Dobie might

bite. The last group the bulldogs, are not as mean as

Dobies Bulldogs act mean and tough, but if you don't show

fear when they get bossy they will back down. This type

needs to feel in charge, even if it's me leading them

around on a leash.
```

Revising and Editing

After writing her first draft, Vera began revising her paragraph. To revise is to rearrange and polish the writing, putting the sentences in the best possible order and coming up with the best possible words. Vera used the acronym CLUESS to remember her revision checklist.

Coherence: Does the material flow smoothly from each idea leading logically and evenly to the next?

Language: Are the words appropriate for the message, occasion, and audience (avoiding slang, clichés, and worn-out expressions)?

Unity: Are all the ideas related and subordinate to the topic sentence?

Emphasis: Are techniques such as repetition and careful placement of words and ideas used to emphasize the main points?

Support: Do details, examples, and similar material back up, justify, or prove the topic sentence?

Sentences: Is there some variety in sentence structure? Have fragments, comma splices, and run-ons been corrected?

Finally, Vera edited her paper. To edit is to correct the basic writing errors that have been overlooked. Vera used the acronym COPS to remember the one question that would cover her concerns.

Are there problems with capitalization, omissions, punctuation, and spelling?

Here is Vera's first draft, revised and edited.

Customers Are Like Canines

language
punctuation

Over the years while working
~~I have worked~~ in a beauty salon∧ ~~for a~~

~~long time. There,~~ I have come across almost

every kind of salon customer, each with her

sentences   own unique looks and personality. *Because* I am also a

dog lover and I have observed numerous dogs

punctuation   with care∧ it is easier to classify these

language   people if I *relate them to* ~~compare them with~~ canine types—

logic   but in a playful rather than a mean way. The

first group is made up of poodles. Poodles

language   are very prissy, *and high-strung* with a constant need for

attention. Their hair is usually over styled.

They think puffballs in soft colors look

great. The *last* ~~next group~~ and largest group, is

emphasis
spelling   made up of cocker spani*e*ls. The C/ockers are
omission

very lovable *and* the most faithful. They *enjoy* ~~like~~

language   being ~~pampered~~ *groomed and stroked, but they are easy to please.* Cockers like to see me every

week and *to* visit with others. Sometimes I can

almost see their tails wagging. Then come the

sentences   Doberman pinchers. *This type scares me the most. Dobies are hard to please. If one hair

sentences   goes the wrong way, I will see their upper lip

language   rise up to ~~show~~ expose eyeteeth, ~~as if they are~~

~~snarling.~~ I rarely turn my back while working

punctuation   on this type; a Dobie might bite. The ~~last~~ third

group members, the bulldogs, are not as mean as Dobies.

language   Bulldogs act mean and tough, but if ~~you don't~~ one doesn't

punctuation   show fear when they get bossy, they will back

down. This type needs to feel in charge, even

language   if ~~it's me~~ I'm leading them around on a leash.

No matter what, canines and customers are my best friends.

Here is Vera's final draft:

Customers Are Like Canines

topic sentence   Over the years while working in a beauty salon, I have come across almost every kind of salon customer, each with her own unique looks and personality. Because I am also a dog lover and have observed numerous dogs with care, it is easier to classify these people if I relate them to canine types—but in a playful

support   rather than a mean way. The first group is made up of poodles. Poodles are very prissy and high-strung, with a constant need for attention. Their hair is usually overstyled.

They think puffballs in soft colors look great.

support Then come the Doberman pinschers. This type

scares me the most. Dobies are hard to please.

If one hair goes the wrong way, I will see

their upper lip rise up to expose eyeteeth. I

rarely turn my back while working on this type—

support a Dobie might bite. The third-group members,

the bulldogs, are not as mean as Dobies.

Bulldogs act mean and tough, but if one doesn't

show fear when they get bossy, they will back

down. This type needs to feel in charge, even

support if I'm leading them around on a leash. The

last—and largest—group is made up of cocker

spaniels. The cockers are very lovable and the

most faithful. They enjoy being groomed and

stroked, but they are easy to please. Cockers

like to see me every week and to visit with

others. Sometimes I can almost see their tails

wagging. No matter what, canines and customers

are my best friends.

✳ The Writing Process Worksheet

The guide on page 202 may be useful in helping you move from assignment to the final paragraph or essay. Your instructor may ask you to enlarge the page on a photocopier, complete it, and submit it with your final paper. It can direct you through the stages of writing and show your instructor how you proceeded.

Writing Process Worksheet

Title _____

Name _____ **Due Date** _____

Assignment   In the space below, write whatever you need to know about your assignment, including information about the topic, audience, pattern of writing, length, whether to include a rough draft or revised drafts, and whether your paper must be typed.

Stage One   **Explore**   Freewrite, brainstorm (list), cluster, or take notes as directed by your instructor. Use separate paper, if you need more space.

Stage Two   **Organize**   Write a topic sentence or thesis; label the subject and treatment parts.

Write an outline or a structured list.

Stage Three   **Write**   On separate paper, write and then revise your paragraph or essay as many times as necessary for co-herence, language (usage, tone, and diction), unity, emphasis, support, and sentences (**CLUESS**). Read your work aloud to hear and correct any grammatical errors or awkward-sounding sentences.

Edit any problems in fundamentals, such as **c**apitaliza-tion, **o**missions, **p**unctuation, and **s**pelling (**COPS**).

202

✳ Common Paragraph and Essay Patterns

After you write a strong topic sentence or thesis, you need to decide on a framework for the development of your paragraph or essay. Divide your treatment into parts; what the parts are will depend on what you are trying to do. Just consider the thought process involved. What sections of material would be appropriate in your discussion to support or explain your topic sentence or thesis?

The following are among the most common forms of division:

- Divisions of time or incident to tell a story

  I. Situation
  II. Conflict
  III. Struggle
  IV. Outcome
  V. Meaning

- Divisions of example or examples

  I. First example
  II. Second example
  III. Third example
  (or divide one example into three or more aspects)

- Divisions of causes or effects

  I. Cause (or effect) one
  II. Cause (or effect) two
  III. Cause (or effect) three

- Divisions of a unit into parts (such as a pencil into eraser, wooden barrel, lead, and point)

  I. Part one
  II. Part two
  III. Part three
  IV. Part four

- Divisions of how to do something or how something was done (such as obtaining ingredients and utensils for *preparation* and doing the cooking according to *steps*)

  I. Preparation
  II. Steps
     A. Step one
     B. Step two
     C. Step three
     D. Step four

✳ A Variety of Writing Topics

Here are some paragraph and essay topics. For each topic that you choose, try one or more prewriting techniques, such as brainstorming, freewriting, or clustering. Then develop a strong topic sentence and a clear outline before you write, revise, and edit your paper.

1. Write about one event that took place in no more than five minutes. Perhaps it had a special meaning as a discovery, reason for change, or transformation. It could be outstanding because of the pain, pleasure, or insight it gave you.
2. Write about the best or the worst decision you made during the past three years.
3. Write about the breakup of a relationship. Concentrate on causes or effects.
4. Discuss a problem on campus, such as registration, class schedules, counseling, student activities, or parking. Use specific examples of the problem and suggest a solution.
5. Write about people's driving habits that bother you. Give some real-life examples.
6. Bring in a newspaper article of opinion (often located on the page facing the editorial page) or a letter to the editor and then agree or disagree with it in a very specific way.
7. Write your own letter to an editor of a newspaper about an issue in the news. Consider mailing your letter.
8. Write about needed changes in procedures, management, products, or services in your workplace.
9. Write about an imaginary vacation to a time and place of your choice in world history (no space-alien abduction pieces unless approved by your instructor).
10. Imagine that you have just won a million dollars in the lottery. Explain what you would do. Be specific in naming products and beneficiaries.
11. Write your job description (what you are supposed to do) in one paragraph, explaining each task as a part of your total job, and then, in an additional paragraph, explain what you really do.
12. Discuss a personal hero or role model. Emphasize the important qualities of that person.
13. Argue for or against school uniforms or a restrictive dress code for a particular high school. Refer specifically to apparel.
14. Explain the significance of body piercing and/or tattooing to a typical mainstream person over forty.

15. Summarize a passage from a college textbook. When you summarize a passage, you rewrite it, making it shorter by about two-thirds, changing the wording without changing the information, and concentrating on main ideas. Do not add ideas, refer to yourself (by using "I"), or give your opinion. Begin by underlining the important ideas and annotating the printed material. Then construct a simple outline. Try referring only to your outline to avoid the temptation of copying material.

16. Write a detailed account of how someone helped you at a time when your self-esteem was low.

17. Write a narrative about the first time you did something, such as the first time you dated, kissed romantically, spoke formally in public, entered a new school, worked for pay, drove an automobile, rode a bicycle or motorcycle, danced, received a traffic citation, met a celebrity, or played a game.

18. Write a narrative about a personal experience that you might characterize as the most amusing, sad, terrifying, satisfying, stupid, rewarding, self-centered, generous, stingy, loving, thoughtful, cruel, regrettable, educational, corrupting, sinful, virtuous, or disgusting thing you have done or witnessed. Keep in mind that you are writing about a single event or a portion of that event.

19. Write a paragraph about the effects of disease (a particular disease, perhaps on just one person), fighting (one or two people involved in a dispute), fire (a particular one), alcoholism (a certain alcoholic), getting a job (a person with a particular job), early marriage (a person who married very young), teenage parenthood (one person or a couple), or dressing a certain way (one person and his or her style).

20. If you are from an immigrant family, write about what happened when your family learned about American culture by watching television soon after you arrived in this country.

21. Write about the effects television watching has had on you. How has your life changed by the amount of TV viewing you do and by your choice of programs? This topic will be especially revealing if you have a television-free segment (a time when you did not watch television) to compare with a television-watching segment.

22. Use the Internet to research the price, quality, style, and durability of two items that are for sale. Make copies of your data. Write a comparison and contrast paper explaining that one item is better than the other. Submit the computer printout along with the materials required by your instructor.

23. Write an argument either for or against the practice of using cameras in classrooms to help control bullying, cheating, bad teaching, and thefts.

24. Discuss an occasion when you changed your opinion of something or someone.

25. Write an account of someone who was unable to deal with stress. Your case study can come from something you either witnessed or heard about at home, work, or school.

26. Imagine you are leaving a job without being able to give notification. Your respected—and understanding—boss asks you to write out instructions in short essay form to help your replacement perform a task.

27. Write about a workaholic (a person who places work above all other activities and concerns) you know. Emphasize either the effects on that person and his or her family or the causes of the person's becoming fanatical about work.

28. Write about an occasion when you or someone you know did something that was daring and out of character.

29. Use one extended example of someone who is a good boss, worker, parent, coach, spouse, or neighbor.

30. Write about a crime, an accident, or a natural disaster you witnessed.

✳ Index